Unveiling Unbelief

Sandi Burris

Table of Contents

Acknowledgement

I want to acknowledge Jesus and His Lordship over my life and this assignment. I am in awe that God has allowed me to write in book form one of the many wonderful revelations He has given me to preach to His people. Given my background, it still amazes me that God has called upon me to write this book. It should be proof to all that if you have *"faith as a grain of mustard seed, all things are possible!"*

God has carefully hand picked a group of people who have helped me to develop this project. He is faithful to equip us with what we need to accomplish His work at exactly the right time. I have discovered, throughout this process, where I lack, God has caused someone else to step in with the knowledge and expertise to finish the job. **Romans 12:5** says, *"So we, being many, are one body in Christ, and every one members one of another"*. We are each one members of His body and each one equipped with different skills supplying the needed wisdom and understanding to bring the task to completion. Some have joined the team in recent years and some have been by my side from the beginning.

Thank you, with sincere love and appreciation to my husband, Jerry Don who spoke to me regarding this book in its earliest stages. They were simple words spoken on an *uneventful day*. Those simple words have urged me on during *very eventful days* filled with accusations from the enemy of my inadequacies and inabilities. I also want to acknowledge my beautiful daughters, Kimberly, Kourtney, and Kristee-Camille. No one knows the sacrifices my family has made for the ministry. I do not know if they or anyone else understands what all of them mean to me. Thank you, Jerry Don and my precious girls. I love you so. I would not be who I am if all of you were not who you are.

Thank You to Angela Sutton, who worked tirelessly and selflessly to help in any and every way. If nothing else, to call and say, *"I believe in you and I love you"*. It was encouraging to hear someone say, *"Helping you has helped me"*.

Thank you to Pastor David Craig, a son in the faith, who wrote me letters of encouragement. His words were to me as spurs digging deep into the fleshy flanks of a horse bred to run. Although the fitly spoken words he penned made me wonder why I was the one writing this book, not him; yet they spurred me on to the finish line no matter how close or far away that line appeared. His Bible based encouragement built me up in a powerful way that equipped me for the spiritual warfare that was to come.

Thank you to Levenda Cosby, who contributed much in proofreading and reconstruction. She drew knowledge from wells of education and expertise that I had not to draw from. Her contribution was priceless as well as selfless.

Thank you, to all those who have encouraged, proofread, and prayed for the birthing of this book.

Last, but not least, thank you to my gorgeous, five year old, granddaughter, Madyson who believes and has convinced me that her Grand Mother Dear can do anything, including when she grows up and has a baby, talking the doctor out of giving her a shot. Madyson, your love and admiration for me have been a glistening light on many dark days. I love you.

Sandi Burris

About the Author

There is a cry in the Body of Christ for genuine, Christ-centered, Spirit-filled ministry: ministry that is not self-promoting and ego driven. The cry is for ministers, who walk with God, hear His voice, and speak on His behalf; ministers whose lives so completely belong to God that evidence of His ownership is displayed in their public and private lives.

Sandi Burris is one such gift to the Body of Christ. Her consistency in prayer and fasting results in a life of contagious faith that spreads like wild fire everywhere she goes. Oliver Wendell Holmes is quoted as saying, *"Once a man believes there is better ahead, he can never go back"*. God has ruined Sandi by showing her that there is certainly *better ahead*. She has experienced the substance of this hope in her own life, and is now driven to ignite all of us with this fire of faith. Her ministry pulls back the curtain and points to the beautiful horizons that await those who dare to live by faith.

In the Old-Testament, the prophet Samuel, demonstrates the strength of a man who could rebuke King Saul to his face, coupled with the tenderness to then fall on his face and weep for Saul. Few are able to balance the lion and lamb attributes of Christ without leaning toward extremes. Sandi Burris is one such person. Decades of ministry travel and selfless service across our nation and abroad have exposed Sandi to both the heroes and the casualties of the journey.

With fresh revelation from God, giving evidence of her many hours of prayer and fasting, Sister Sandi always delivers a bold message to the Body of Christ. A spirit of excellence is a hallmark of this great ministry. She raises the standard of how the church should carry itself in these days of opportunity. God has entrusted her with a powerful, prophetic anointing that has proven trustworthy and accurate. Among the many voices of our day, she is a true voice from God. God has chosen to validate her message and her ministry with signs and wonders through the years. Deliverance from demonic possession, healings, miracles, breaking of generational curses, and many unique signs have followed this ministry.

God has favored this lady to reach into diverse cultures with great success. She is not a one-dimensional preacher. She seems to know how to handle every situation that arises in ministry and in life with a grace and dignity befitting the family of God.

Sandi Burris is not only a vessel of honor that God is using across the nation behind the pulpit, but she is a shining example of character, integrity, and virtue that the Body of Christ needs to see.

The years of ministry have not diminished her flame or weakened her constitution. Sandi's ministry burns with the passion of urgency toward man and obedience to God.

The pages of **"Unveiling Unbelief"** are wet with ink from the pen of a ready writer that bears the *Word of God* for this generation. **Expect to be changed!**

Introduction

Is something standing between you and your destiny? Are you confident in your heart and mind that you have received direction from the Lord, but cannot seem to progress in that direction? Do you have a vision regarding His plan for your life, but are having difficulty seeing that vision accomplished? Do you have enough faith for victory over some circumstances, but feel as though something is preventing you from reaching the full potential God has placed in you?

If only one obstacle were standing between you and God's ultimate plan for your life, what would you do about it? If the Holy Spirit shed light on the vast darkness between where you are and where you are going, would you turn your back and walk away? Could you?

Would you begin a foot race and quit in the last quarter turn? Would you run the distance only to give up right before you reach the finish line? Would you stand idly by and watch someone else walk away with the prize you had worked so hard to obtain? No, you would not. When you set a goal to finish a race in the natural you expect to be tired, thirsty, trembling, and wracked with pain before you reach your final destination. You train hard, muster determination, and envision victory *before* you begin. You know that reaching the prize at the end will require perseverance. How can you expect spiritual things to be different?

If you have found yourself worn out, burned out, and crying out, do not despair! The Bible says in **Philippians 4:13,** *"I can do all things through Christ which strengtheneth me"*. According to scripture, you have the strength to do *ALL* things through Christ, not some, but *ALL* things! The Lord will help you finish the race He has set before you, if you fully rely on Him. Jesus Christ has already experienced the physical agony and the mental anguish of the race for you. He has already been broken, beaten, and put to death that you and I might finish strong.

Many times people have the misconception that *big* problems standing in the way is the hindrance to what God has called them to be and do. This is not true. It is as simple as your flesh *veiling* the key element to your deliverance. The revelation God has given in ***"Unveiling Unbelief"*** will *unveil* the number one device the devil uses to stop people from reaching their destination and accomplishing God's will for their lives.

I pray that you will take hold of this revelation so nothing stands between you and the plan God has so carefully laid out for your life. If you are determined to possess what God has promised, then you will see how important it is to confront key issues and ***"press on toward the mark for the prize of the high calling of God in Christ Jesus"***! **Philippians 3:14**.

I am reaching out to those who have lost hope and who have fallen into a self-absorbed life style that *can* be changed. I am also reaching out to people who are confused and frustrated because they are doing all they know to do and it does not seem to be working.

There is a devil assigned to your life to keep your destiny out of reach, but Jesus has an assignment for your life, also, and it is more powerful than *any* assignment from the devil. Jesus not only wants you to reach your destiny, but walk in it and enjoy it!

I am reaching out to those determined to go the distance. Rest assured, God has a plan and a destiny for your life that is as unique as you are!

1

FINISHING THE COURSE

DO NOT GROW WEARY

2 Corinthians 5:17

"Therefore if any man be in Christ, he is a new creature: old things are passed away; behold, all things are become new."

When you first commit to the Lord, you are full of hope and expectancy. It is easy to commit to the race before you. As a new creature, you are full of newfound faith. Optimistic and ready to take on any assignment for the Lord, you are confident the devil has met his match. Having joined forces with the winning team, you set out at a mind-numbing pace.

After a while, though, difficulties are bound to come and you may question if you are on the right track. You are beginning to feel the effects of the race. You are committed and making progress, but you begin to tire and your flesh begins to rebel. You begin to wear out, burn out, and cry out. Racked with pain and running desperately, you long to reach your destination. If only you could stop and rest for a while and think the whole thing through. If only you could suspend time long enough to gather your thoughts, plan a new strategy, and refresh yourself a bit, but that is not how you run a race. Once the race begins, you must see it through.

Spiritually, it is the same. You are in the race to your destiny. Now is no time to give up. You *must* not start second-guessing God. You *must* not stop until you cross the finish line. You must press on and finish the course set for you from the beginning. The time to stop and look around comes when the race is over. Only then can you look up to see how well you finished.

Galatians 6:9

"And let us not be weary in well doing: for in due season we shall reap, if we faint not".

If you have received direction from the Lord regarding your life, but the race you are running more closely resembles a hamster on an exercise wheel, it is time to re-evaluate.

If you are tired and it seems impossible to finish the race and reach your destiny, you should look at what might be hindering your progress. If you feel as though you may never see the *Word of God* bear fruit in your life, *be encouraged.* If hopelessness and despair are causing you to feel it is impossible to step into your destiny, you need to know there *is* an answer.

DESTINY DEFINED

What is **"destiny"**? One dictionary definition refers to *"destiny"* as *"the seemingly inevitable succession of events; one's fate"*. Many people think this means they have no control over their lives; whatever happens, good or bad, will simply happen. *"Que Sera, Sera"*. What will be will be. *WRONG!* Another dictionary definition refers to **"destiny"** as *"intended for purpose"*. Keep this definition in mind as you read the word **"destiny"** throughout this book.

EACH ONE of you has a God-given vision, purpose, and destiny. Not everyone is called to the five-fold ministry (*apostles, evangelists, pastors, prophets, and teachers*), but all are ministers to the people they meet on a daily basis. You may rest assured that God has a destiny (*intended purpose*) and plan for your life that is as unique as you are. This destiny, however, will not be accomplished inevitably or uneventfully. The devil is the enemy of your soul, and he delights in delaying, or stopping you from reaching your destiny by using adverse circumstances and events in your life. The following pages will *unveil* the number one obstacle the devil uses when attempting to impede your destiny.

THE "OBSTACLE"

UNBELIEF is *the* obstacle you must conquer in order to find the answers for the trouble in your life. It is the one thing holding many back. If not for *unbelief*, they would move forward into the destiny God has revealed to them. Could *unbelief* be holding you back?

Have you ever claimed healing or victory for one problem only to see deliverance elude you in another area? Many times people experience a certain amount of victory, but find at least one area in which they experience little or no victory.

One thing is holding back many ministries, hindering families, and affecting worship. One thing is at the root of your inability to press in and finish the race to which God has called you. That one thing is *UNBELIEF*.

Learn to recognize *unbelief TODAY!* Begin to develop the necessary type of faith to deal with and remove *unbelief*. If you do, you will be empowered to overcome any problem. If you truly desire to fulfill God's plan for your life, rid yourself of *unbelief*, move forward, and reach your destiny, examine the following scripture. Herein lies the answer.

Matthew 17:20

". . . for verily I say unto you, If ye have faith as a grain of mustard seed, ye shall say unto this mountain, Remove hence to yonder place; and it shall remove; and nothing shall be impossible unto you."

Jesus instructs His disciples in **Matthew 17:20** they need *"faith as a grain of mustard seed"*. Jesus is teaching His disciples that with *"faith as a grain of mustard seed"* or faith that *"acts like"* a grain of mustard seed, they can speak to the mountain and it will move. Then, *"NOTHING"* will be impossible unto them!

You too, must develop *"faith as a grain of mustard seed"* or faith that *"acts like"* a grain of mustard seed and understand that the *mountain* represents **unbelief** in *you*.

There is an anointing for moving forward and finishing the race. Your personal life, family, and ministry need to move forward, but the obstacle of **unbelief** must first be overcome. This can only happen through development of *"faith as a grain of mustard seed"* or faith that *"acts like"* a grain of mustard seed.

Do you have a desire to press in and reach your destiny no matter what it requires of you? Be willing to acknowledge the *unbelief* in your heart. If you do not, you have made the choice to stay on the level of faith you have attained. Your choice will cause you to fall short of or deny your destiny.

How determined are you? Are you willing to do what it takes to fulfill your vision? The choice is yours. Will you choose to move ahead or fall behind? Realize, if you do not choose to move forward, you *will* move backward. There is no way to stay in the same place with God. Any move that is not toward God is away from Him. Do not allow yourself to be guilty of backing away from your destiny. Be sincere about pressing into God's plan for your life. Your destiny will unfold, as you are obedient to His Word.

Be encouraged. Developing *"faith as a grain of mustard seed"* or faith that *"acts like"* a grain of mustard seed is possible. It is a process. Later, you will discover *"The Mustard Seed Process"* which will explain in depth why Jesus likened mountain-moving faith to a *grain of mustard seed.* Once you understand and yield to this process, your *"faith as a grain of mustard seed"* or faith that *"acts like"* a grain of mustard seed will mature and you will produce results for the *Kingdom of God.* Developing *"faith as a grain of mustard seed"* and eradicating *unbelief* is all it takes to finish the race and reach your destiny. Then, *"NOTHING shall be impossible unto you"*!

Understand; you have a choice. Only you can decide to evaluate your personal life, family, and ministry. You, and only you, are responsible for the *Word of God you* hear and what you do with it. You are responsible for the enlightenment you receive. The only person who can make the choice is you.

Choose to move forward with new revelation and insight into God's Word. Understand you will reach your destiny much sooner if you do. Take hold of the *Word of God* and apply the truths and principles therein. Promise yourself you will apply and put into practice these truths as He reveals them to you, and you *will* see major change. Your personal relationship with the Lord will deepen and become more intimate and you *will* fulfill the vision God has given you.

It does not matter whether you received your Word from the Lord last week or twenty years ago, how long you have been a Christian, or how many times you have failed in any particular area. The obstacle standing between you and your destiny is a mountain of *unbelief* and the only way to move that mountain is by developing *"faith as a grain of mustard seed"* or faith that *"acts like"* a grain of mustard seed. Then you can *speak* to the mountain of *unbelief* and it will move!

GOD CONTROLS DESTINY

Proverbs 5:21

"For a man's ways are in full view of the Lord, and he examines all his paths." (NIV)

Until now, you may have looked at God's vision from your perspective only. Catching only a glimpse of the vision, you began planning your route. You did not realize, however, that the route you planned would never take you to the place God has promised. Follow *His* plan, because He is the One who has full knowledge of where He is taking you.

If you tell your young and impressionable children you are taking them on a picnic, you can be sure they will be excited and ready to *BE* there. They have some idea what to expect, but they are oblivious to the amount of preparation it takes for a picnic. You do not arrive instantly at the park with your blanket spread and your picnic basket full. You *must* go through a process and prepare before you get there. You *must* know which items you need, which direction to go, and the amount of travel time. Fuel stops must be taken into consideration, because if you set out with the idea of traveling a lengthy trip non-stop, you will likely wind up on the side of the road out of gas.

Sometimes it takes only a short time to get where God is taking you, but sometimes it takes months, *EVEN YEARS!* God knows the way. He knows what you need along the way, where you need to stop, and which direction you should go. Be patient. Use wisdom and caution as you may run into road construction, detours, or delays, but *do not* give up. You set out with a destination in mind and you *will* reach it.

God sees your entire course from beginning to end and He knows what it will take to get you where you are going. The road that makes the most sense to *you* is likely *NOT* the one God will use. God allowing you to plan the route to your destiny would be like allowing your young children to plan the picnic. Although eager and filled with desire, they do not have the knowledge or experience to take control of such a task and see it accomplished. If your small children were in control of the trip, how far would you get before you made a wrong turn, ran out of gas, or broke down? Would your picnic basket contain all the items needed? Would you have enough money and fuel to reach your destination? Likely not!

Children lack the maturity to plan and carry out this kind of trip and it would be disastrous to allow them to try. You are God's child and it would be *as* disastrous for Him to allow *you* to take control of your destiny. Only God can get you there!

If the choice were yours, you would choose the expressway straight to your destiny. No interference and no delays. No fuel stops, oil checks, or food breaks. If you were in control, you would go from salvation to nationally known TV Evangelist or from apprentice to

CEO immediately, but it does not happen that way. If you do not stop to check God's map, you will lose your way. If you do not pay attention to those who have gone before you, you will not realize a detour is needed because the road is out ahead. If you do not stop to refuel yourself with God's Word, you will waste away before you get to the destination God has planned for you.

When things are not moving fast enough and you desire to take control of your journey, stop and look around. Ask God to help you see and appreciate the place where you are at this present time. Ask Him to reveal to you how far He has brought you. Surrender your will and desires and allow Him to take full control of this journey. God knows exactly where you are going, and He knows the best route that will take you there!

AUTHOR AND FINISHER OF YOUR FAITH

The Bible tells us Jesus is the *"author and finisher of our faith"*. **(Hebrews 12:2)** An author is *"one who promotes, originates, or creates"*; a finisher *"develops or brings something to completion"*.

Jesus is the Author and Finisher (*or developer*) of ALL faith, but we are talking specifically about *"faith as a grain of mustard seed"* or faith that *"acts like"* a grain of mustard seed. Jesus is the one who will create in you *"faith as a grain of mustard seed"* needed to *"finish"* or *"develop"* the vision God has given and rid you of the mountain of *unbelief.*

The process of *"finishing your faith"* is much like the process of developing a photograph. The process by which photographs are developed begins with a blank piece of film in a dark box or camera. Rays of light enter the camera and are focused into an image. In traditional photography, light exposes the film in the camera, causing chemical changes on the surface of the film. After the film has been exposed, it goes to a darkroom to be developed. During development, the areas of film receiving more light appear dark on the film and the areas receiving only a little or no light appear light or clear. This produces a reversed image on the film. A piece of coal would appear white on the film and a snowball would appear black. The developed film is called a *negative* and looks exactly the opposite of the finished picture.

Film is a sheet of special paper or plastic with a coating over it. It is highly sensitive to light and undergoes changes when exposed to light. The degree of change depends on the amount of exposure. The light the film is exposed to will vary in intensity. Light-colored objects reflect much light, and dark colors reflect little or no light. Chemical changes produce an image on the film that can barely be seen, containing all the details for the finished photograph.

As with film in a camera before exposure, you start out in darkness, total darkness. You are born with a sin nature and must be saved by the blood of Jesus. When you are born again, you are similar to exposed film. In a flash, you are exposed to the light of the life of Jesus Christ, but that is not the end. After exposure, begins a process of development that eventually produces a finished product for all to see.

Like the negative, you contain the *image* of the finished picture. In the natural, it would seem as though this is as far as you will go. You underwent change after exposure to the light of Jesus, but that change is only an outline, barely discernable to the naked eye. Although you see only an outline, you have hope. Everything you need for the finished product is already in place. You need only to go through the developing process in order to become what God has said you will be. You already have within you *EVERYTHING* you need. If you continue the developing process, the finished product will portray all the details God intended. If you allow *"faith as a grain of mustard seed"* or faith that *"acts like"* a grain of mustard seed to develop, you will become the perfect representation God has created you to be.

As you read the following chapters, disregard conventional thoughts and ideas you may have regarding the path to your destiny. God will place people and situations in your path to teach, encourage, test and correct you in order to bring you into the likeness of Him.

He will use whatever means necessary to develop *"faith as a grain of mustard seed"*, or faith that *"acts like"* a grain of mustard seed in you, because this type of faith is the faith needed to finish the course.

2

ENVISIONING THE VISION

GOD GIVES VISION

Habakkuk 2:2-3

"And the LORD answered me, and said, Write the vision, and make it plain upon tables, that he may run that readeth it. For the vision is yet for an appointed time, but at the end it shall speak, and not lie: though it tarry, wait for it; because it will surely come, it will not tarry."

Thank God for vision in your personal life and ministry! *Vision* is *"a supernatural appearance that conveys a revelation"*. *Vision* is the Rhema Word spoken to you by revelation from God. The

Hebrew word *"marah"* is translated *vision* and means *as seeing something in a mirror or appearance.*

God's people are not without vision. Many men and women of God are preaching prophetic messages all over the world. God is speaking through His servants to deliver a message of hope to those who are running toward their destiny. Those in the race have caught a glimpse of what God has in store, but many have yet to see that image materialize.

For many, the problem is not lack of vision, but lack of seeing vision *accomplished* in their life, family, or ministry; year after year, looking to the same vision, standing on the same Word, but seeing no change. They are talking the same talk, doing the same things, and believing the same prophetic word, but *nothing* changes.

Know this; God gives you vision in order for vision to be accomplished. He does not give you vision to tease you with blessings you cannot have or taunt you with tasks you are unable to complete. He gives you vision to accomplish His purpose and His will. Though finishing your race may be taking longer than you anticipated, you can be sure, God's plan will be fulfilled in His time. The vision He has placed within you *will* manifest.

Everyone, no matter what the spiritual level, social class, or economic background, has *purpose*. Reaching your destiny is impossible for you alone, but it is well within God's ability. In Him and through Him, you are more than able to do all He asks you to do.

2 Timothy 1:9

"Who hath saved us, and called us with a holy calling, not according to our works, but according to his own purpose and grace, which was given us in Christ Jesus before the world began."

God has called us with a holy calling *"not according to our works"* but *"according to his own purpose and grace"*. Be sensitive to the Holy Spirit and press in to the principles of God in order to see His plan accomplished in *each* area of your life. Continue looking toward the vision and know you are called according to God's *purpose*.

VISION FOR MINISTRY

When you first receive a Word from the Lord for your ministry, you are eager to see the Word bear fruit. Convinced God will bring transformation within twenty-four hours, your expectations are high. Sometimes things transpire quickly. Some ministries burst forth into their promise, going from one level to another so quickly it is amazing. However, the vision may be longstanding and what is actually seen is the fruit of much prayer and faith development. The process may have been lengthy and unseen, but the materialization of the promise draws the attention.

While one ministry catapults into its destiny, another may seemingly remain on the same level for many years. Some ministries have waited for years and not seen the change and growth God has promised. Year after year, they hold tight by faith to a vision that remains just out of reach. They are unable to progress beyond a certain point.

Arriving at the place God has revealed as their destiny seems impossible. A great deal of time may be spent in revival meetings, outreaches and conferences, but little progress is made. They struggle for years using every avenue to promote growth, but while some growth is experienced, there is also a falling away. They may experience a tremendous move of the Spirit one service and barely feel a pulse in the next.

It is not *unbelievers* experiencing these problems. It is born-again, Spirit-filled Christians in all types of ministry who have trouble reaching the destination they *know* God ordained. They have simply not realized there is a mountain of *unbelief* standing between them and their destiny.

These ministries remain stuck in a pattern they repeat year after year. The devil has them caught in a trap, always looking back. Tied to a stake with an imaginary rope, they keep going round and round, freedom and fulfillment just beyond their grasp. Each time around, it wears a rut that gets deeper and deeper.

For the most part, each pastor, deacon, elder, lay member, Sunday school teacher, youth minister, evangelist, music minister, etc. desires to walk in the promise they know God has given for their ministry. Why then, does it happen for some, but not for others?

Sin in a ministry will cause problems and stunt the growth of the ministry, but what happens when this is not the case? Sometimes you spend a great deal of time looking for some gross sin when the problem is the tiny molehill of *unbelief* rising up from within.

Keep in mind, God operates outside of time. When it takes longer than expected for God to act, do not allow the devil to move in and take advantage of situations and circumstances. His endeavor is to distract you from the vision and keep your focus on the time it is taking to reach your destiny.

Those in ministry rarely begin with the spiritual maturity to manage the position God desires to place them in. It takes time to develop the skills needed to finish the race God's way. God's promises are woven into lives, and the flesh is brought into submission so that it does not hinder His plan. As this happens, spiritual growth comes, areas of *unbelief* are *unveiled* and ***"faith as a grain of mustard seed"*** or faith that *"acts like "* a grain of mustard seed is developed.

Take hold of the vision God gives and do not be deterred. Allow Him to expose areas of *unbelief* in your ministry. No matter how long it takes, remain faithful to God, knowing He is faithful and will bring about His promise for your ministry in due time.

VISION FOR MARRIAGE

Vision is different from dreams and expectations. Vision for marriage is *the* destination *GOD* wants to take the both of you, not where *YOU* want to go.

Christians sometimes assume, equally yoked, godly marriages, will be free of complications. They marry with hope and expectation of living *"happily ever after "*. They share a belief in prayerful communication, financial prosperity, perfect children, and flourishing families. Thoughts of disagreement, adulterous affairs, or divorce never enter their minds. Their thoughts are focused on a unified prayer life, work in the church, and rearing their children to love and serve God with their whole heart, mind and strength.

However, many factors must be considered. Though the marriage is part of God's plan, this is a life-long commitment to someone you barely know. There will be an adjustment period. Careers and family life add to the scenario and when you begin blending families it can be tricky. It does not take long to realize constant prayer is a necessity to make all of the pieces fit properly.

Though you have sought God for a spouse, and are convinced beyond all doubt this person is part of God's vision, there will *still* be problems. Circumstances beyond your control can arise to hinder a marriage relationship such as, baggage brought in from previous experiences that have nothing to do with this one. There may be financial difficulties, illness, disability, or death. Any or all of these events can take an emotional toll and cause you difficulty in a marriage relationship. Any one of these situations can build a mountain of *unbelief*, leaving you feeling unsure of God's ultimate plan.

A completely new set of circumstances arises when one party falls into sin. Some have experienced situations such as out-of-control anger, broken trust, adultery, drug addiction, or alcoholism. When things of this nature take place in a relationship, they can cause hopelessness. A mountain of *unbelief* will form and cause you to stop believing there is *any* life in the vision God gave. You may see no possible solution to the problems you face. You may wonder if you have somehow missed His plan for your life; but this is not the case.

Sometimes people look at marriage from a *"dream state"* and not from a realistic view of what marriage is. This automatically sets them up for a mountain of *unbelief* to form. Marriage is a relationship, and like any other relationship, it has times of difficulty. There are good times and bad times; times of happiness and times of sadness; times of success and times of failure. Every working relationship contains a little of all these things. If your spouse starts *cuttin' up* and loses sight of the vision, make sure you *tighten up* your grip and keep it ever before you. Set yourself to see the salvation of the Lord in this area. Nothing less than success is acceptable. Purpose to seek God and continue to move by faith into your destiny together, trusting Him to give answers as He sees fit.

God knows each of you intimately. He knows exactly the right combination of personalities and temperament necessary to work in each of you what He desires. The level you allow God to operate and control your life determines how many times you repeat the test and when you move on.

When you contemplate the scripture **Proverbs 27:17,** *"Iron sharpeneth iron; so a man sharpen the countenance of his friend"*, does it sound like an easy process? No. I doubt that anyone who has a marriage that has survived broken trust, adultery, addictions, or abuse, will tell you it was easy to overcome and keep their focus on God's overall plan for their lives, but it can be done.

God has a plan for your marriage. Practice forgiveness and patience and refuse to allow a mountain of *unbelief* to form. If you continue to seek the Lord with your mate and/or for your mate, God will continue to lead you in the direction of your destiny.

Perhaps, as you read this, you are single. Are you believing God for a mate? When you look at the world, it is easy to lose hope of finding someone with whom you will be *"equally yoked"*. Yes, even Christians can have trouble finding the right person with whom to spend the rest of their lives. There is such demonic activity in the world that simply attempting to build a godly relationship is a difficult process.

Whether young or old, meeting someone new can cause great anxiety, and committing to a life-long relationship can be frightening. You may have the desire for a godly mate but the difficulties you experience and the fear associated with the search may make you feel as though you will *never* find someone. Many lose hope in their vision for God's perfect mate for them and decide to settle for a bad relationship or no relationship at all. *This* is an indication a mountain of *unbelief* is forming.

Whether you have been married for years, never married, divorced, or widowed, God has a plan for you. Entrust your life and your relationships to Him and know He will provide you with exactly what you need when you need it. This includes the right mate. Do not allow a mountain of *unbelief* to form regarding the choosing of a godly mate. Keep praying and focusing on God and allow *Him* to bring you the person He desires. This is the only way you can be sure the marriage will work and you will reach the destiny God has planned for you both.

VISION FOR FAMILY

A family is defined as *"the basic unit in society traditionally consisting of two parents rearing their own or adopted children".* In a time where single parent families, extended families, and blended families are common, it becomes easier to lose sight of God's vision for the family.

Proverbs 22:6

"Train up a child in the way he should go: and when he is old, he will not depart from it."

Individuals may differ in the details of what they would like to see accomplished in their families, but for the most part, Christians share a common desire – to have peace, unity and spiritual growth in the family. Christian parents desire to see children saved and all family members working in whatever call God has placed on their lives. The desire is that they choose a lifestyle of holiness and live their lives *with* integrity and *without* compromise.

Families are made of individuals and therefore, it is very important that each family member grasp the common plan of God for the group as a whole.

In these last days, very few families are defined by the *"traditional"* definition of family. Some homes consist of blended families *(or two broken families combining to make one).* Some families consist of one parent with children due to divorce, death or other causes. All of these make up unconventional family structures and affect how you view God's plan for your lives as a whole.

In some families, whether biological, adoptive, foster, or stepparents, there is a lack of knowledge to give proper spiritual training. Unsaved or unskilled parents may unknowingly send mixed signals that confuse their children with inconsistent lifestyles.

If you have a situation where only one parent has Jesus Christ as Lord of their life, there is added trouble. One parent lives by the world's standards and one parent by God's standards and unfortunately, children often times prefer the lax ways of the world to the discipline of God's plan for them; but do not lose heart.

Children hear what you tell them, but more importantly, they see what you do! You must be careful not to cause a mountain of *unbelief* to form in the lives of your children or family members due to *your* disobedience to God. An unconventional family structure or other problems will not alter God's plan for your family. He will see His vision accomplished. If you do *your* part to follow godly principles, God will do the rest.

Matthew 12: 46-50

"*While he yet talked to the people, behold, his mother and his brethren stood without, desiring to speak with him. Then one said unto him, Behold, thy mother and thy brethren stand without, desiring to speak with thee. But he answered and said unto him that told him, Who is my mother? and who are my*

brethren? And he stretched forth his hand toward his disciples, and said, Behold my mother and my brethren! For whosoever shall do the will of my Father which is in heaven, the same is my brother, and sister, and mother."

Have family members rejected you because you are too involved in the things of God? Do they think you are too *"fanatical"* or *"preachy"* about your beliefs? Do you have a desire to see your loved ones come to the Lord, but they seem to be more focused on what you are *not* doing for them than on what they *should* do for Christ? Whether or not you realize it, many people suffer the greatest amount of anguish, agony and ridicule from those they love the most, members of their own families!

If this describes your situation, you are not alone. Remember, according to **Matthew 12:46-50**, Jesus' family was upset with Him when He did not stop to talk with them. A multitude of people was eager to hear Jesus teach, but His mother and brothers wanted to speak with Him.

This passage of scripture **(Matthew 12:46-50)** raises a couple of interesting questions. Why was His mother not next to Him in the first place? Why were His brothers not His most faithful disciples? Jesus was delivering the *Word of God.* His enemies were watching, hoping to catch Him in some wrongdoing, and His family was placing even more pressure on Him! You would think *they* would be His biggest supporters!

You cannot force family members to see what you see, or know the things you have come to know. They do not have the revelation you have. Continue to pray for them and intercede (*"stand in the gap"*) for them.

God may allow certain circumstances in the individual lives of your family or in the family structure to shape and mold them into His image. It may be difficult to understand how these situations fit into God's plan, but you must rely on Him and trust Him to bring those family members into the Kingdom. Seek God for the accomplishment of His vision in your life *and theirs*. You will stand before Him to give account for your life, and they will give account for their lives. No other person will answer to God for how you use what you have been given. You must not allow your desire or vision for your family or their lack of desire or vision to build a mountain of *unbelief* in *you*. This will delay *you* in reaching *your* destiny.

Matthew 10:37

"He that loveth father or mother more than me is not worthy of me: and he that loveth son or daughter more than me is not worthy of me."

In order to reach your destiny, you must choose to follow God's plan. If you choose others above Him, the Bible says you are not worthy of Him. Forsake ALL others if that is what it takes. This is a hard thing, but may be required if you truly want to reach your destiny. Do not choose *anyone* or *anything* above God. You must not choose the approval of your family. You must not be in bondage to a desire for love and acceptance of flesh and blood. If you intend to finish the race, continue with God regardless of circumstances. Allow *Him* to bring others into their destiny.

If your marriage, family, or ministry is not yet experiencing the *fullness* of its vision, do not give up. God gives vision that it might be accomplished. He does not go back on His word. The Bible says in **Ecclesiastes 7:8,** *"The end of a matter is better than its beginning, and patience is better than pride".* Hold fast to your vision and allow God to take you into your destiny.

TALKING AND NOT WALKING DESTROYS VISION

Do you talk about making changes in your life but never actually experience true change? Do you wonder why you remain defeated by the same negative behavior year after year? Are you frustrated because you cannot rid your life of anger, strife, disappointment, depression, fear, or hopelessness? These questions may sound familiar to many of you. The problem is, merely *talking* of making changes is not enough to produce them. You must confront the obstacle keeping you from implementing the desired changes. That obstacle is *UNBELIEF*. Understand that no change will take place in your life until you deal with *unbelief.*

Maybe it is difficult for you to have **"faith as a grain of mustard seed"** or faith that *"acts like"* a grain of mustard seed because other people around you have lived defeated lives. Pastors, friends, parents, or others may have allowed *unbelief* to cause them to fail. If you follow their example, you may feel it is impossible to succeed and overcome in order to see desired changes. It is imperative for you to understand the *real* problem is *unbelief* and *YOU MUST RID YOURSELF OF IT!*

You cannot *change* what you will not *confront*! The enemy uses fear of confrontation and fear of failure to keep you from confronting negative things working in your life. People often think of confrontation as being between them and another person, but you must confront the personal issues *within you* that are hindering *you*. Lack of confrontation causes you to doubt things can be different. In turn, *unbelief* causes you to continue only *talking* about changes instead of actually implementing them.

Have you ever wondered why you cannot lay hold of the answer and press into God's principles? Have you ever questioned why you can find the time to do the things you want to do, but never seem to have time for God? Maybe you desire a more fervent prayer life and more knowledge of the *Word of God*, but you have failed to incorporate these things into your life. It is not enough to *know* you need to change, and it is certainly not enough to *talk* about change. You must confront your *unbelief* and develop **"faith as a grain of mustard seed"** or faith that *"acts like"* a grain of mustard seed to produce action and accomplish change. Come to the place where you exercise self-control and self-discipline, and give God what is His. Consider tithing your time to God. To *"tithe"* is *"to give a tenth part of"*. If you tithe your time, you will find situations coming in line with the *Word of God* very quickly.

CONTROL AND MANIPULATION DESTROYS VISION

God should control your life, not people. Allowing a spirit of control and manipulation to reign is dangerous. It can operate through any person. It will work through co-laborers in the ministry, children, other family members, or your closest friend if allowed. This spirit will involve anyone vulnerable to its deception. Controlling relationships will cause you trouble in *all* areas of your life and will *stop* your progress in the race to your destiny. A spirit of control and manipulation will adversely affect your job, friendships, family, and ministry causing a mountain of *unbelief* to form.

The spirit of control and manipulation may lay dormant and go undetected, until you begin to take ground toward your destiny. It is an antagonizing spirit and if allowed will antagonize you. When this spirit sees you begin to move forward, it will rise up to prevent you from doing so.

People entertaining a controlling spirit are in rebellion and may influence you to rise up against leadership. They will underhandedly build a case against leadership. When the people involved become upset with leadership, this spirit will rise up and manifest in a number of ways. Before long, it will reach into the lives of others in ministry with you. This spirit will come against authority of any kind and will encourage others to do the same. When this happens, the ministry is in danger of shipwreck.

Someone controlled by this spirit will do everything within their power to tear down the things God has used you to accomplish. They are often so demanding and set on getting their way, they will form a campaign to destroy an entire ministry-its integrity, influence and finances. Not only does the spirit of control and manipulation affect the life of the person entertaining it, it can have a ripple effect.

These individuals delay not only *their* destiny, but also the destiny of others.

If you determine to continue on the path to your destiny in spite of opposition from a controlling spirit, you will be attacked brutally and repeatedly until you do one of two things, cave in or overcome. You *MUST* overcome!

It is idolatry to allow yourself to be controlled and manipulated by people rather than be obedient to God. You may think of idolatry as worshiping an inanimate object, but the definition of idolatry is, *"the worship of a physical object as a god, or the excessive attachment or devotion to something"*. If you are *excessively* attached to anyone or anything, including family members, this is idolatry. When you idolize people, disappointment is certain. Disappointment will cause a mountain of *unbelief* to form.

This spirit is especially difficult to deal with when the people involved are family members. You can be especially vulnerable where your children are concerned. It is possible to be so controlled by your child that you forsake your destiny in order to appease the child. If a child (*or any person*) rises up and demands your attention above the Lord, do not pull away from Him and His will, to pacify that individual. If you do, *unbelief* will begin to infiltrate, bringing you to a place of concession and defeat.

Recognize when your children and others truly have needs, but also recognize when they have agendas that will hinder your progress. You may appear to be progressing in the direction of your destiny, but still be affected by the relationships that are based on another person's selfish desires. If you do not deal with the spirit of control and manipulation, it stands to hinder you and everyone close to you. Pray for release from the influence of those with whom you share this type of relationship. Take authority over controlling and manipulating spirits in any relationship. Bring them under the blood of Jesus Christ. That is where spirits are truly dealt with.

You must not let go of close relationships out of frustration, aggravation, or agitation. If you are at odds with people, ask God to remove the blinders from your eyes where they are concerned. You must *release* these relationships to God by faith and let Him deal with them. Continue to obey Him and move forward in the call He has placed upon *your* life.

You have a responsibility to encourage people in their walk with the Lord. God has a vision for their life, also. Work with them and help them discover their destiny and call but do not allow a controlling spirit to manipulate you. Do not allow another *person* to dictate your choices. You cannot deem their needs greater than the call God has placed on you. Doing this would place you in danger of delaying *your* destiny.

REBELLION DESTROYS VISION

Rebellion will destroy your vision. Rebellion will affect every area of your life: prayer, unity, Bible study, and peace. Rebellion may find a place in you, a spouse, a child, or some other individual close to you.

Those in rebellion have the attitude *"it's all about ME".* Rebellion causes a selfish, self-centered, self-absorbed thread to run through people of all ages. Those in rebellion feel the world *owes them*. Their golden rule is *"do unto others **before** they do unto you"*.

At some point, *you* may struggle with rebellion. There is a push and pull between God's desires and your flesh. God has a plan for your life *but* Satan will try to entice you. Rebellion is deceptive and everyone is tempted to rebel at some point. You may notice it first in your toddler, then in your teenagers. You may not see it as clearly in adults, but it rises up in people of all ages given the right set of circumstances.

Rebellion has many facets and is manifested in different ways. Drugs, alcohol, and premarital sex are readily available to young people. Peer pressure and natural desires entice them. Teenagers are pulled in the direction of these things, by their flesh, because they appear fun. The devil paints such a pretty picture of sin in the beginning, but know this . . . *". . . the wages of sin is death;"* **Romans 6:23.** It is only after they are caught in the devil's trap that they realize sin is not as glamorous as it looks. There is nothing glamorous about drug addictions, alcoholism, teen pregnancy, disease or incarceration.

Take authority and stand against the devil's influence. Rebellion may be accepted as *"normal"* and it may be considered *"fashionable"* in today's society, but it must be guarded against. There is such a *"tug of war"* in the lives of many by Satan. You must communicate with spouses and children, ever mindful of the example you are; *practice what you preach.*

Keep this in mind; rebellion by *one* will make *trouble* for *many*. The devil sets up circumstances that cause *unbelief* and destroys your vision. If you talk about God's plan for your life but do not walk in it, it will destroy your vision. Allowing a spirit of control and manipulation to function will destroy your vision. Guard against giving in and giving up in these situations. Allow God to take complete control of what you become and when and how you reach your destiny.

3

FATHOMING FAITH

WHAT IS FAITH?

Hebrews 11:1

"*Now faith is the substance of things hoped for, the evidence of things not seen.*"

What is faith? Faith is defined as *"allegiance or duty to a person, fidelity to one's promises, sincerity of intentions, belief, trust and loyalty to God, belief in traditional doctrines of a religion, firm belief in something for which there is no proof, complete trust"*.

Faith means you *BELIEVE* in spite of your inability to confirm the existence of a thing. You cannot see it or touch it, but you know it is there. Faith is the *opposite* of *unbelief.*

Matthew 9:27-29

"And when Jesus departed thence, two blind men followed him, crying, and saying, Thou son of David, have mercy on us. And when he was come into the house, the blind men came to him: and Jesus saith unto them, Believe ye that I am able to do this? They said unto him, Yea, Lord. Then touched he their eyes, saying, According to your faith be it unto you."

In **Matthew 9:27-29**, two blind men followed Jesus crying out for mercy. Jesus asked these two men if they believed He could heal them, and they said, *"Yea, Lord"*. As He touched their eyes, He said *"According to your faith be it unto you"*.

Matthew 9:30

"And their eyes were opened."

This verse says the men's *"eyes were opened"*. In the natural, their physical eyes *literally* opened and they saw, their spiritual eyes opened as well. When Jesus said it would be done unto them *"according to their faith"*, there must have been an instant revelation. *IF YOU DOUBT, YOU DO WITHOUT!*

Place yourself in this same situation. If Jesus said to you today that you could have your miracle according to the development of your faith right now, would you be victorious? Would you see your promise come to pass?

Let us look at faith from four different levels: "Teeny-Weeny Faith", "Plain, Old, Ordinary Faith", "Overcoming Faith", and *"faith as a grain of mustard seed"*. All of you probably know someone with each type of faith. If you know someone who has *"faith as a grain of mustard seed"* in their arsenal of spiritual weapons, then you know the necessity of developing this kind of faith for yourself.

All faith is beneficial and productive, and any type of faith will gain some victory. If you have little faith, you receive small victories, but to be truly victorious and conquer *unbelief,* you must have *"faith as a grain of mustard seed"*. Without *this* kind of faith, *unbelief* will attempt to seize your every thought, endeavoring to devour you with torment. With *"faith as a grain of mustard seed"* or faith that *"acts like"* a grain of mustard seed, your thoughts will be illuminated with the revelation that NOTHING shall be impossible for you.

Maybe you are aware of the type of faith you are walking in right now, or maybe you have never given it much thought. As we give explanation to these different types of faith, realize you need to have *"faith as a grain of mustard seed"* or faith that *"acts like"* a grain of mustard seed in order to reach your destination and see your promise fulfilled.

"TEENY-WEENY FAITH"

Matthew 14:23-33

"And when he had sent the multitudes away, he went up into a mountain apart to pray: and when the evening was come, he was there alone. But the ship was now in the midst of the sea, tossed with waves: for the wind was contrary. And in the fourth watch of the night Jesus went unto them, walking on the sea. And when the disciples saw him walking on the

sea, they were troubled, saying, It is a spirit; and they cried out for fear. But straightway Jesus spake unto them, saying, Be of good cheer; it is I; be not afraid. And Peter answered him and said, Lord, if it be thou, bid me come unto thee on the water. And he said, Come. And when Peter was come down out of the ship, he walked on the water, to go to Jesus. But when he saw the wind boisterous, he was afraid; and beginning to sink, he cried, saying, Lord, save me. And immediately Jesus stretched forth his hand, and caught him, and said unto him, O thou of little faith, wherefore didst thou doubt? And when they were come into the ship, the wind ceased. Then they that were in the ship came and worshipped him, saying, Of a truth thou art the Son of God."

Do you sometimes start out strong but begin to sink when the storms of life rage? This is characteristic of "Teeny-Weeny Faith". This kind of faith will get you somewhere you have never been before, but it will take *more* than this kind of faith to propel you into your destiny.

Peter said, *"Lord, if it be Thou"*. Do not miss this; Peter believed. Peter had faith. At least he had the courage to climb down out of the boat! If you listen closely to his speech, however, you can detect a bit of doubt. He believed; but it was dark, windy, and rainy. He said, *"Lord, IF it be Thou, bid me come unto Thee on the water,"* and he climbed down out of the boat and started in Jesus' direction. Before he got there, though, he began to sink. Peter lost his focus. He took his eyes off Jesus and began to look at the surrounding circumstances.

Doubt arose and his "Teeny-Weeny Faith", though strong enough to get him *out of the boat, in a storm,* was not strong enough to take him to his desired destination.

You, however, must set *your* heart to develop *"faith as a grain of mustard seed"* or faith that *"acts like"* a grain of mustard seed, if you want to finish your race and reach your destination. *Always remember, little faith is not rejected, but great faith or faith that accomplishes great things is commended.*

"PLAIN, OLD, ORDINARY FAITH"

You can operate fairly well with "Plain, Old, Ordinary Faith" for short periods of time as long as life does not present too many strong storms. As long as you are planted in good ground with few obstacles, you will grow. You will bear sumptuous fruit as long as the frost does not come and you will flourish as long as the weather is fair. You have faith that God will take care of you and see you through *until* something major happens. As advantageous as "Plain, Old, Ordinary Faith" is, it will eventually run into an obstacle it cannot surpass and give up.

"Plain, Old, Ordinary Faith" will get you some victory; but you should keep on pressing, pressing, pressing until you have developed *"faith as a grain of mustard seed"* or faith that *"acts like"* a grain of mustard seed. If you are reading this, you desire spiritual growth. You are looking for something more than "Plain, Old, Ordinary Faith". You sense things happening underneath the surface, but you might not be able to *see* the work God is doing yet. Continue to press in, and

He will develop *"faith as a grain of mustard seed"* or faith that *"acts like"* a grain of mustard seed in you.

"OVERCOMING FAITH"

Some of you have "Overcoming Faith". You may have a battle in a particular area of your life and have not seen victory in that certain area, but it does not mean you do not have "Overcoming Faith". In most situations, you know the Lord is at work on your behalf, and circumstances do not rock you. You hold steady. In other cases, you have to fight death, hell, and the grave to stay on your feet. In these areas, the devil has found an open door and has set up a stronghold. Be encouraged! I want you to know the strongholds of the Holy Ghost are infinitely more powerful than the strongholds of the devil!

Sometimes you lose sight of your "Overcoming Faith" because you focus on one area in which you have not yet attained victory. Do not allow the devil to seize your attention and cause you to focus on this one area. In order for God's plan for you to come to fruition (*a pleasurable state of bearing fruit*), you must deal with *unbelief*. You must develop *"faith as a grain of mustard seed"* in order to experience victory in ALL areas.

"FAITH AS"

Matthew 17: 20

"And Jesus said unto them, Because of your unbelief: for verily I say unto you, If ye have faith as a grain of mustard seed, ye shall say unto this

mountain, Remove hence to yonder place; and it shall remove; and nothing shall be impossible unto you."

Jesus said, *"if ye have faith as a grain of mustard seed."* Undoubtedly people have interpreted this to mean that if you have a little bit of faith, you can move literal mountains. That is not what the Bible says. The Bible says if you have *"faith as a grain of mustard seed"* or faith that *"acts like"* a grain mustard seed, you can move this mountain (*unbelief*) and nothing shall be impossible unto you. If you have *"faith AS a grain of mustard seed"*, you can speak to the mountain of *unbelief* and it *"shall remove"*. In addition, NOTHING shall be impossible unto you.

Notice, too, Jesus said *"if"* you have *"faith as a grain of mustard seed"*. He said *"if"*, because there is a decision to be made. You have a choice. You can have faith and it not be *"faith as a grain of mustard seed"* or faith that *acts like* a grain of mustard seed. Jesus said *"Be it done unto you according to your faith"* - your "Teeny-Weeny Faith", your "Plain, Old, Ordinary Faith", your "Overcoming Faith" or your *"faith as a grain of mustard seed"*. You can have different types of faith, but He said if you have *"faith as a grain of mustard seed"*, you can speak to the mountain of *unbelief*, and nothing shall be impossible unto you.

ABRAHAM STAGGERED NOT

Romans 4:17

"Abraham staggered not at the promise of God through unbelief; but was strong in faith, giving

> **glory to God. And being fully persuaded that what he had promised, he was able also to perform.**"

When you think about people of faith, one of the first to come to mind is Abraham. When first you read of Abraham, his name is Abram. Remember, earlier we discussed the process your faith goes through. It is like the developing of a picture. You could say Abram was in the *"negative"* stage of his development. God had not yet changed his name to Abraham. Abraham would not only go through a name change, but also many other changes before he reached his destiny. Abraham did one crucial thing; *HE BELIEVED.*

God told Abraham to leave his people, his father's house and his country to go where He showed him. It must have looked like an impossible journey, but *he believed* and away he went. God took him through the land of Canaan and told him his seed would inherit the land. At that time, the Canaanites inhabited the land. It looked impossible, but Abraham *believed.* God told Abraham He would make him a great nation beginning with a child from his own body. It looked impossible, but Abraham *believed.* God told Abraham to look up at the heavens and count the stars. God told Abraham, **"So shall your offspring be"**. It looked impossible, but Abraham *believed.*

Genesis 15:6

> **"And he believed in the LORD; and he counted it to him for righteousness."**

Abraham did not consider the uncertain journey. He did not consider his age. He did not consider that his wife Sarah was past childbearing age. He simply *believed* what God said and that God was able to do what He said He would do. This alone was enough for God to count Abraham righteous or to place him in *RIGHT STANDING* with Himself.

Abraham did not have to know how or when his promise would manifest. Most of all, Abraham did not have to *make* it happen! The only thing God required Abraham to do, he did. He *BELIEVED*! Abraham was from the wrong family, the wrong country, and the wrong religion. With all odds against him, he made up his mind to believe God, and *that* was all God required.

Choose to believe God as Abraham did. When the fulfillment of your vision looks impossible, allow *"faith as a grain of mustard seed"* or faith that *acts like* a grain of mustard seed to be developed, through whatever process God chooses. Abraham believed God in spite of circumstances or obstacles. He believed if God said it, He would *perform* it and He did. God always keeps His end of the bargain. He always does what He promises. Remember *your* responsibility. You must *BELIEVE!*

As your *"faith as a grain of mustard seed"* or faith that *"acts like"* a grain of mustard seed is developing, step into obedience. If you truly believe, you will obey. God will test your faith by asking you to step out and obey *before* you see anything in the natural. This can be the dividing line between faith (*knowing God can*) and *"faith as a grain of mustard seed"* (*knowing no matter what, God will*). As you are about to see, Abraham had *"faith as a grain of mustard seed"* or faith that *"acts like"* a grain of mustard seed. When placed in the ultimate position of testing, his *faith* served him well.

Genesis 22:1-3

"And it came to pass after these things, that God did tempt Abraham, and said unto him, Abraham: and he said, Behold, here I am. And He said, Take now thy son, thine only son Isaac, whom thou lovest, and get thee into the land of Moriah; and offer him there for a burnt offering upon one of the mountains which I will tell thee of. And Abraham rose up early in the morning and saddled his ass, and took two of his young men with him, and Isaac his son, and clave the wood for the burnt offering, and rose up, and went unto the place of which God had told him".

Abraham did not question God when told to sacrifice his promised son. If he desired confirmation, he did not voice it. He simply saddled up, took two men, a bundle of wood, his *only* son of promise, and embarked on the journey.

Neither Abraham nor Isaac knew exactly what was about to take place. Abraham assured Isaac that God would provide. Abraham **BELIEVED** God. Abraham had waited on this son for twenty-five years. God had provided this promised son, and Abraham believed God was in control of the situation facing him now. Could he see the outcome? No. Were there any guarantees God would intervene? No.

God had taken many things from Abraham in the beginning, but for everything He took, he always gave back better. God took

Abram's name and gave him the name *"Abraham"*. God told him to go from his fathers house and leave his country and God gave Abraham Canaan.   God took Abraham away from his religion as a moon worshiper and gave him righteous faith.   For everything God took from Abraham, He gave him back more in order to multiply him. God had promised Abraham his seed would be as the sand on the seashore and Abraham was confident that if God took his only son of promise it would be for the purpose of multiplication.

Abraham could have been distracted or erred at this point. God had added to him a son, Isaac. Changing your name, switching religions or moving across the country was surely difficult, but sacrificing your only son of promise? Abraham knew only that God had never failed to multiply what had been subtracted from him. Now was not the time to allow *unbelief* to intimidate.

God's ultimate promise was to multiply Abraham, but as with everything else in Abraham's life, he had to start with the basics: addition, subtraction and finally multiplication.

When you first learn addition and subtraction, it lays a foundation for multiplication. You no longer need to add several things together one at a time. It becomes simpler to multiply those items. With God, multiplication will not come if you do not first allow Him to add to and subtract as He sees fit.

God added to Abraham a son. He then asked Abraham to release that son to Him. It was essential that Abraham obey. Only then would God multiply his seed as He promised. Abraham knew to do precisely as God had said. There was no other option.

Genesis 22:13-15

" And Abraham lifted up his eyes, and looked, and behold behind him a ram caught in a thicket by his horns: and Abraham went and took the ram and offered him up for a burnt offering in the stead of his son. And Abraham called the name of that place Jehovah-Jireh: as it is said to this day, In the mount of the Lord it shall be seen." With resolve, Abraham proceeded with the plan to sacrifice his son. In the final moments, as he raised the knife to slay Isaac, an angel of the Lord stopped him. Then, and only then, did Abraham see the ram caught in the thicket by its horns."

Abraham called the place *"Jehovah-Jireh"* meaning *"Jehovah-Sees"*. By divine revelation, Abraham knew, *"God Sees"* everything. God saw that Abraham obeyed immediately in beginning his journey. God saw that Abraham did not withhold his only son. God also saw the emotional pain Abraham experienced. Abraham received a revelation that no matter where you are or what you are going through, **God Sees**. Abraham also had another revelation. With the revelation that *"God Sees"* came the revelation, *"the Lord will provide"*.

You *must* get this revelation! When your back is against the wall and there seems to be no way out, **God Sees!** Even though your faith may be underdeveloped, God *sees* your willingness to obey. God's nature is so giving that when He *sees* your faith and obedience, He is compelled to provide. When you obey, know this; God has your miracle tied up by the horns in a designated thicket. You cannot see it, but God knows right where it is.

At first, Abraham did not see his miracle. It was in the thicket. A *"thicket"* is a *"dense or impenetrable growth of shrubbery"*. The dictionary also uses the word *"tangle"* to define thicket. This means that Abraham's miracle was *"hidden behind"* or *"tangled up in"* the dense growth. His miracle was being *hampered* yet *held*, by this tangled, confused mess. This is testimony that God uses the tangled, confused messes in life to produce miracles.

God's immediate provision for Abraham was a ram with its horns caught in a thicket, but there was much more. God told Abraham since he had not withheld his only son, He would bless him and multiply his seed as the sand of the sea and the stars of the sky. This same God *sees* your need and has made provision for you. Be obedient; step into faith; and claim **ALL** God has for you!

Faith as . . .

4

AS THOU HAST BELIEVED

THE POWER OF AUTHORITY

Matthew 8:5-10

"And when Jesus was entered into Capernaum, there came unto him a centurion, beseeching him, And saying, Lord, my servant lieth at home sick of the palsy, grievously tormented. And Jesus saith unto him, I will come and heal him. The centurion answered and said, Lord, I am not worthy that thou shouldest come under my roof: but speak the word only, and my servant shall be healed. For I am a man under authority, having soldiers under me: and I say to this man, Go, and he goeth; and to another,

> **Come, and he cometh; and to my servant, Do this,**
> **and he doeth it. When Jesus heard it, he marveled,**
> **and said to them that followed, Verily I say unto you,**
> **I have not found so great faith, no, not in Israel."**

In this passage, a centurion, a man of authority as well as a man under authority, came to Jesus and explained that his servant was sick. Jesus agreed to go and heal him. The centurion knew the power of the spoken word of someone in a position of authority. Not only did he recognize that Jesus was a man of greater authority, he also knew Jesus need only speak the Word and his servant would be healed.

The centurion had a revelation many of us need. This man believed that by speaking from a position of authority Jesus could heal his servant. Jesus recognized this man's exceptional faith, because the Bible tells us *"Jesus marveled"*. Jesus was so impressed with this man's faith He turned around to the ones following Him and told them, *"I have not found so great faith, no, not in Israel"*. **(Matthew 8:10).** What a powerful statement! Many people had so little faith, yet this man did not need to *see* to believe. He understood authority and exactly what it took to get things done.

Matthew 8:13

> **"And Jesus said unto the centurion, Go thy way; and**
> **as thou hast believed, so be it done unto thee. And**
> **his servant was healed in the selfsame hour."**

Jesus tells the centurion, *"Go thy way, and as thou hast believed, so be it done unto thee – and his servant was healed."* As *thou hast believed.* Do you have this kind of faith? Do you have the kind of faith to walk away and know it is *done*? If the things you asked for were given to you *"as you believe"*, would you experience miracles? Would you have all your prayers answered? Would you have financial blessings in your life? Are your *belief, trust, and loyalty* to God strong enough to believe in a spoken word? If Jesus told you to go your way and it would be done unto you, *as you believed*, would your miracle come in the self-same hour?

You must be as the centurion. He believed Jesus could heal his servant by merely speaking. This man had a revelation of the authority of Jesus. The authority Jesus exercised could not be seen, yet the centurion was confident of the power behind it.

Who told this man about Jesus' authority? Had he heard of the miracles Jesus was performing, or did he simply recognize power and authority when he saw it? Maybe it was a combination of both, but he saw results. Jesus seeing how great his faith was told him to *"Go thy way, and as thou hast believed, so be it done unto thee."*

This centurion was exercising *"faith as a grain of mustard seed"*. His faith was strong in the authority Jesus used to perform these miracles. He may not have known all the details of how it would happen, but he knew Jesus did. He believed what Jesus *said* would be *accomplished.* That is all that was required to receive his miracle.

FAITH THAT MAKES JESUS MARVEL

Would your *faith* make Jesus marvel, like the centurion's or would you be like those in **Mark 6:1-6** who caused Jesus to marvel at their *unbelief*?

Mark 6:1-6

"And he went out from thence, and came into his own country; and his disciples followed him. And when the sabbath day was come, he began to teach in the synagogue: and many hearing him were astonished, saying, From whence hath this man these things? and what wisdom is this which is given unto him, that even such mighty works are wrought by his hands? Is not this the carpenter, the son of Mary, the brother of James, and Joses, and of Juda, and Simon? and are not his sisters here with us? And they were offended at him. But Jesus, said unto them, A prophet is not without honour, but in his own country, and among his own kin, and in his own house. And he could there do no mighty work, save that he laid his hands upon a few sick folk, and healed them. And he marveled because of their unbelief. And he went round about the villages, teaching."

These people could not get past their familiarity with who Jesus was, where He came from, and who His family was. They found it hard to believe that Jesus, a carpenter, could do these miracles. Could Mary's son do these mighty works and have such wisdom? They wanted to know who He thought He was. Jesus, knowing they could not accept Him, tells them plainly, *"A prophet is not without* honour, but in his own country, and among his own kin, and in his own house". (Mark 6:4).

Matthew 13:58

"And he did not many mighty works there because of their unbelief."

Jesus did not do many mighty works there because of the *unbelief* in the people. He was God and possessed the power to perform miracles, but if He had, there was so much *unbelief* they would probably have reasoned the miraculous acts away. They would not have given credit where credit was due. Do you see what *unbelief* does to the work of God? *Unbelief* hinders you and can literally stop a miracle from happening by allowing doubt and *unbelief*.

Jesus went throughout the region teaching instead. After all, *this* was acceptable to people in that area, and you must deal with people on their level. If people are not on the level to agree with you for your vision, do not share it with them. If they cannot stand with you in *"faith as a grain of mustard seed"*, believing in spite of all circumstances that you will attain your vision, do not open your heart and pour out your precious treasure to them.

If you allow it, a mountain of *unbelief* can form in the area of familiarity with other people. When people are familiar with you, they know all of your shortcomings and flaws. They know your background and the mistakes you have made. When you are familiar with people, you are aware of their faults also. This *knowledge* can be a hindrance to the development of *"faith as a grain of mustard seed"* on both sides. They may question how God could possibly use *you* to be His ambassador. A mountain of *unbelief* can also form if *you* focus on *their* shortcomings and cannot look past them to see God's vision for their life. Accept people on the level of revelation *THEY* have and proceed in *your* work for the Lord. Jesus did exactly that.

BE CAREFUL WHAT YOU HEAR

Romans 10:17

"So then faith cometh by hearing and hearing by the word of God."

The Bible says in **Romans 10:17**, *"So then faith cometh by hearing . . ."* Be careful what you hear. Faith comes by hearing and hearing by the *Word of God*. If you listen to negative comments from other people, you may begin to doubt your vision and be hindered from reaching your destiny. This hearing is not the kind of *"hearing"* that builds faith. Realize others have not heard what you have heard from God. Your vision is your vision; your destiny is your destiny. **Romans 10:17b** says, *"and hearing by the word of God"*. Whatever is revealed to you as you read your Bible and what you hear from God should be the determining factor in the works *you* do for the Lord. Do not allow people to determine what you are and where you are going.

YOU WILL BELIEVE IT WHEN YOU SEE IT

You may not be able to see the fulfillment of your vision from where you are now. God promised your ministry would grow, but you may feel as though you are losing ground. God promised your business would prosper, but the financial flow is obstructed. God promised to save your lost family members, but in spite of hours of intercession, they seem determined to live their lives in opposition to God's ordained purpose. God promised you promotion and advancement, but you lack the necessary education, and do not know how you will succeed. You know what God promised, and you know the word He spoke to you, but short of a miracle, you cannot see any way for the promises to be fulfilled. Under the circumstances, your attitude is, *"I will believe it when I see It"*.

Hold on just one minute! God is a miracle maker! He performs miracles daily. God performs financial, spiritual, physical and emotional miracles. God gives favor in unfavorable situations. He qualifies with His glory. He literally makes a way where there seemeth to be no way. Yes, you *have* seen the promises of God manifested. Why is it that even now you do not believe? Why do you continue to ask God for confirmation of your vision and *proof* of your promise? Why keep asking for one more miracle and one more sign *before* you believe? The Bible clearly says in **Mark 16:17** *"And these signs shall FOLLOW THEM THAT BELIEVE; In my name shall they cast out devils . . ."* You *must* **believe.** If God said it, He will do it, but first you must deal with your mountain of *unbelief.*

Mark 16:20

"And they went forth, and preached everywhere; the Lord working with them, and confirming the word with signs following. Amen."

In **Mark 16:20** the disciples *"went forth and preached everywhere"*. The Bible plainly says the Lord was working with them, confirming the Word with *signs following*. The signs followed and confirmed the Word; the Word did not follow the signs. *First* believe and *then* see.

Begin to pray, read, study the Bible and meditate on what God has spoken to you. Do not focus on circumstances. God may use situations that *appear* to be totally opposite from the direction of your destiny. As you are obedient to God and follow His direction for your life, you will see evidence of His plan unfold. You will begin to see how circumstances work together to lead you in the direction God wants to take you.

When God speaks to you, *act* on the Word He gives. *THEN* you will *see* the confirmation you need. As you move in this vein, your faith will grow and you will *see* God open up the windows of heaven, rain down blessings, and bring forth the promise He has spoken to your heart. The *"see it"* will follow the *"believe it"* according to God's Word.

GOD'S FAITHFULNESS DOES NOT FAIL

One of the most important things to remember is that in your strength, you can do nothing. All that is good is poured into each one of you *from* God to be poured out again *for* God. You are merely vessels.

Romans 3:3

"For what if some did not believe? Shall their unbelief make the faith of God without effect?"

Understand this, you have a choice. You can develop *"faith as a grain of mustard seed"*, or faith that *"acts like"* a grain of mustard seed or you can choose not to. You can speak to the mountain of *unbelief* in your life, or you can choose to let it stand. You also have a choice about how others who do not believe in your vision affect you, but your *unbelief* or theirs does not alter God's *ultimate* plan.

God is faithful; He is all-powerful; and he is in control. God will accomplish His will *even if* you disqualify yourself. After all, He will use any vessel who will allow him to use them. You are the one who will suffer great loss if you choose to remove yourself from the race.

Hebrews 4:11

"Let us labour therefore to enter into that rest, lest any man fall after the same example of unbelief."

Realize the effort it will take on your part not to stumble into *unbelief.* To labor means, *"expenditure of physical or mental effort. You* must labor to finish the race to your destiny. *You* must be cognizant and not embrace *unbelief. You* must be conscious of the mountain of *unbelief* as it forms in your life and deal with it.

God has a perfect plan for your life, but you can refuse to walk in it. How much better it is to totally surrender yourself to the tender mercies of *Almighty God.* Yield yourself to God and allow Him to mold and make you as He sees fit.

Allow God to develop *"faith as a grain of mustard seed"* or faith that *"acts like"* a grain of mustard seed in you so you will not fall short of fulfilling your destiny.

CONFESS UNBELIEF

Mark 9:23-24

"Jesus said unto him, If thou canst believe, all things are possible to him that believeth. And straightway the father of the child cried out, and said with tears, Lord, I believe; help thou mine unbelief."

Struggling with *unbelief* does not mean you are on the wrong track or that you are condemned to failure. You are human, and humans sometimes struggle before attaining victory. Thank God, you are not in this struggle alone! Be honest with yourself and the Lord and accept that you need help. Do as the man in **Mark 9:23-24**, and ask the Lord to help you deal with your *unbelief.*

Hebrews 4:15

"For we have not an high priest which cannot be touched with the feeling of our infirmities; but was in all points tempted like as we are, yet without sin."

Jesus laid aside the magnificence of heaven and stepped into earth as a man of flesh-and-blood. While on earth, Jesus faced temptation as the son of man, not as the Son of God. Jesus understands that you deal with emotions and negative thoughts. He understands every temptation that comes your way and the difficulty of each moral choice you make. He understands your struggle with *unbelief.* He knows and understands **EVERYTHING** about you. Jesus has given you the power you need to confront the devil and overcome all obstacles in your life, including *UNBELIEF.* Remember, ***"Greater is He that is in you than he that is in the world".*** **(1 John 4:4).**

ONLY BELIEVE

Whatever you do in this life will be accomplished in one of two ways: *naturally* or *spiritually.*

It does not matter what you acquire in the natural—houses, land, money, good-paying jobs, relationships with influential people, prestige—you will still be lacking. Anything you acquire in the natural is only temporary; it will not last.

Mark 11:24

"Therefore I say unto you, What things soever ye desire, when ye pray, believe that ye receive them, and ye shall have them."

In this scripture, Jesus tells you how to receive the things you desire. *Believe* you receive them and you shall have them. He did not say you would have what you desire based on your credit report. He did not say acquiring what you want was based on how good you are at fund raising or how many people are on your ministry team. He did not say you could receive what you want if your children cooperate or if you have a great career or know the *right* people. No. Jesus said if you *BELIEVE* you will receive the things you desire. That is it!

Mark 9:23

"...all things are possible to him that believeth."

To ascend or rise from the natural into the spiritual realm, where problems are overcome, you must first deal with the mountain of *unbelief*. Then, ALL you need do is *BELIEVE*. That is it; *ONLY BELIEVE!* When you have dealt with this mountain, you can *BELIEVE* yourself out of poverty, depression, and disease. You can *BELIEVE* yourself into prosperity, soundness of mind, and good health. You can *BELIEVE* yourself straight into the destiny God has for you. *ALL* you have to do is BELIEVE. To him who believeth, *ALL THINGS* are possible. It does not matter if you do not have one other resource within your reach. If you *BELIEVE*, you have the *ONLY* resource you need!

5

UNDERSTANDING UNBELIEF

UNBELIEF DEFINED

Unbelief is defined as *"a mental rejection of something as untrue, especially in matters of religious faith"*. You may think *unbelief* is not present in you, particularly if you are a Bible believing Christian actively serving the Lord. You go to church, pray, read your Bible, and tithe faithfully. You are benevolent and consistently mindful of those less fortunate. You liberally give offerings to assist those in need. How could *unbelief* be a part of your life?

Unbelief is deceptive. It manifests in ways hard to recognize. *Unveiling unbelief* requires a closer look at everyday issues; because it disguises itself *within* these issues, *unbelief* is often overlooked. When your focus is on the trouble at hand, you may be so consumed with trouble that the root of the problem escapes you. The closer the attack is to you personally, the harder it is to recognize when *you* step into *unbelief*. When trouble is ongoing and circumstances are consistently unfavorable, *unbelief* ensues.

Isaiah 55:8-9

"For my thoughts are not your thoughts, neither are your ways my ways, saith the Lord. For as the heavens are higher than the earth, so are my ways higher than your ways, and my thoughts higher than your thoughts."

Unbelief is not a problem for God. God is *omniscient*. The word omniscient means He has *infinite awareness, understanding, and insight*. It also means He has *complete knowledge* or *is all knowing*. God is also *omnipotent*. This means he has *unlimited authority and influence*. His thoughts are higher and His knowledge and experience are unlimited!

This may be difficult to comprehend. You may feel you have great knowledge of spiritual things, but it is impossible to comprehend an *infinite* God with a *finite* mind. Using human reason to rationalize God's method of operation, will manifest as a mountain of *unbelief*.

If you gave an algebraic equation to a kindergarten student, the problem would not make sense. The child might decide that no answer exists for this seemingly impossible problem. That would be foolishness. A kindergarten student has not been exposed to and would have no way of knowing the real problem was lack of knowledge concerning the subject. The child with its limited exposure to problems of this nature, cannot see the big picture. The key to solving the equation would be gaining more knowledge and experience in that area by way of someone with greater knowledge and understanding of the matter. Given the same equation, a student earning a degree in mathematics, would likely see the problem as elementary. The well-educated student has spent time learning and trusting in the help of those with more knowledge and a better perspective. This is why it is so important to allow God to instruct and develop *"faith as a grain of mustard seed"* or faith that *"acts like"* a grain of mustard seed in you.

Mark 10:27

"And Jesus, looking upon them saith, with men it is impossible, but not with God: for with God, all things are possible."

God has greater knowledge and perspective of your destiny. Difficult situations seem impossible because *you* do not have the knowledge and expertise to devise a solution, but what *you* cannot do is not important. What *is* important is that *NOTHING IS IMPOSSIBLE WITH GOD!* The difficult situations you face must not be allowed to foster *unbelief*, but must be used to build *"faith as a grain of mustard seed"* or faith that *"acts like"* a grain of mustard seed.

RECOGNIZING UNBELIEF

If your desire is to move a mountain of *unbelief*, then you must recognize what causes it to form and how it manifests. Trouble in the church, lack of understanding God's methods, failure of others *(especially Christians),* or *your* blemished background may be reasons a mountain of *unbelief* forms.

Trouble in churches is the *basis* for *unbelief* in many non-believers and is usually a *result* of *unbelief* on the part of some Christians. When there is disharmony or disunity within the church, on-looking non-believers are disheartened by the actions and attitudes of Christians. The *reason* problems occur within the church body is *because* people have allowed *unbelief* to dominate.

Have you noticed that churches have a hard time enjoying fellowship with each other? Many churches have seen a decrease in growth, but an increase in negative things like gossip, slander, and prejudice. Denominational and *non*-denominational lines are drawn boldly. Those attempting to blur these lines may be shunned. Pastors are often reluctant to fellowship with other churches because of fear people from their congregation will move their memberships elsewhere. Individuals might decide they like another church's way of doing things better. They may have a better building, better programs, or they view the other pastor as more attentive or knowledgeable in the *Word of God.*

Some Christians will hold fast to every letter of every doctrine and refuse to fellowship with anyone different from them. Why is this? *Unbelief.* They do not believe, for example, that God will do for them all that He is doing in the church of ten thousand on the other side of the city. They are *afraid* and the root of fear comes from the inability to believe the promises of God. It comes from having a vision but allowing a mountain of *unbelief* to stand in the way of seeing the vision accomplished. If God has promised your church growth into the thousands, then growth will come. It does not matter that you fellowship with many or few, or that people come and go. If you deal with the mountain of *unbelief,* your promise will be fulfilled in God's timing!

When people, especially Christians, cannot flow together in unity, the root of the problem is usually *unbelief.* People have trouble getting along where there is pride or jealousy, and *unbelief* is the root of these two sins. Jealousy says, *I want to be like you, look like you, do what you do, or have what you have.* Being jealous means you do not believe God will do for you all that He has done for another. Jealousy causes you to examine the lives of others under a microscope and to scrutinize their every action. You become extremely critical and begin to pick them to pieces. You are critical of the way they look, the way they wear their hair, how they rear their children, how they treat their husband or wife, how loud they preach, how they pray or do *not* pray, how they prophesy, etc. If left unresolved, intense scrutiny and harsh criticism cause a schism in the body of Christ and prevents people from walking in unity. This is a perfect set-up for *unbelief.*

Seeing other Christians fail is a tremendous cause for *unbelief* in both believers and non-believers. Anytime Christians fail and embrace sin or rebellion there is always someone watching and the watcher is liable to be affected by what they see.

Though the Bible tells us, ***"Judge not, that ye be not judged."*** **(Matthew 7:1),** non-believers do not live by this instruction and when they see a Christian stumble they are quick to judge and condemn.

When other Christians see a fellow brother or sister in Christ stumble, they may lose hope in their own lasting reformation. They may also don a *"religious spirit"* and become judgmental, seeing themselves as *better than* the one who failed.

People are desperate and have enormous problems. They need physical and emotional healing, deliverance for themselves, their children and their loved ones. Restoration of marriages or other relationships and financial blessings are also seriously needed.

People *want* to believe God will follow through with His promises. They desire to see others upholding the standard of the *Word of God* and showing themselves a shining example of Christ. When people fail, as humans do, *unbelief* develops in those who fail and those who witness the failure.

What do you do? How do you resolve these problems? Deal with a mountain. There is a mountain emerging *so* tall you cannot see where you are going. The name of the mountain is **UNBELIEF**! You must believe God and know He is in control! If God has called you to preach, deal with your mountain and preach. If God has called you to prophesy, deal with your mountain and prophesy. If God has called you to the ministry of cleaning the church, deal with your mountain, grab a broom and get to cleaning!

Make sure your heart is right with God! Lay down your pride and believe, *sincerely* believe, in the vision God has given you. Walk in *your* call instead of being jealous of the call of someone else. You will then find yourself happier for your brother or sister in Christ when you see the blessing and favor of the Lord at work in their lives.

BELIEVING GOD WILL DO IT FOR YOU

When you come before God with a need, it may be difficult to believe He will meet *your* need. You know God is able to supply and you believe in miracles. It simply does not seem possible that *you* could experience miracles in *your* life. If you continuously stand in prayer lines and include your name on prayer lists, hoping and praying for answers, but rarely seeing victory, *unbelief* may be forming a mountain. You may not realize you are walking in *unbelief*, but *unbelief* is enough to block your miracle. If it were not for this mountain of *unbelief*, you could pray for *yourself* and be delivered!

As a Christian, you know God sent His Son to save you from a life of misery and eternal damnation. You realize the miracle that is in itself. No one knows better than you how far God has brought you and how much grace He has extended. The awareness of your past may sometimes cause you to feel unworthy. Subconsciously you know God has already gone beyond anything you could *expect* Him to do for you. Maybe you think it a bit presumptuous to assume the God of the universe will reach down and pull you out of your pit of disease, despair, and destruction. He has already done so much for you; how could you ask for more?

Proverbs 3:6

"In all thy ways acknowledge him and he shall direct thy paths."

Are you thinking about the times you have not acknowledged God? Do you doubt that He can bring forth fruit from the mess you have made of your life? You have heard testimony after testimony of God picking someone up and setting them on the right path and making them powerful ministers of the *Word of God*. Would God make a message out of *your* mess? Would He really do that for someone like *you*? Yes, He would!

Your battle is in believing God would use someone who has been an alcoholic, a drug addict, an adulterer, or a backslider. Could someone who has been sexually promiscuous, lied, cheated, or gossiped about others really hope to receive a promise from God? Could they really have a destiny rooted and grounded in Him?

You may feel it is too late to recover your reputation or restore people's confidence in you. For you, it *is* too late; but it is *not* too late for God. You may be one of those snatched from the brink of destruction, sin and rebellion, just before toppling over into the pit. It does not matter what you have done. God will use it for *His* purpose to bring about *His* plan in your life if you allow Him! *Your* testimony will be of God's great grace and love.

Believe God will provide what it takes to receive healing, have financial blessings, preach with boldness, or prophesy under the anointing. How do you do this? Believing for these things takes faith. It takes ***"faith as a grain of mustard seed"*** or faith that *"acts like"* a grain of mustard seed. Ask God to open your eyes and *unveil* the *unbelief* hidden in your life. Ask Him to show you how to *move* that mountain.

You cannot do the things God calls you to do with a mountain of *unbelief* hindering your progress. You *must* believe when you step in front of ten thousand people that God has placed you there, or you will freeze solid. You *must* believe, when God places you in a church of twenty in the backwoods of a place called nowhere, you are doing exactly what He has called you to do or you will become discouraged. You *must* believe God will provide the finances for your ministry or you will place expectations on people that they cannot fulfill and you will walk away disappointed. You know God *can* supply needs, but you must be convinced He *will* supply *your* needs.

QUESTIONING GOD'S METHOD

Be on the look out for *unbelief*! If you find yourself questioning God's method, *unbelief* has *just* been detected.

You know God will do what He promised for others. You want to believe He will do what He has promised you, but you may have found yourself questioning His methods.

Do you feel He would or would not use certain situations to shape you or to fulfill His plan for your life? Maybe you feel insecure without a carefully laid-out map of every step. Do you question God when there are setbacks or detours? These are manifestations of *unbelief*.

Psalm 119:105

"Thy word is a lamp unto my feet and a light unto my path".

When God calls you to accomplish great things, it is never easy. In fact, it is *impossible* for you. If it were possible for *you* to do these things in your own strength, you would do them, but then God would not receive the glory. He does promise, however, to provide a light for your path. Although you may not understand God's method of operation, He continues to have everything under control. What you need to do is move forward in faith, guided by the light of His Word.

GOD DOES NOT CHANGE HIS MIND

Romans 11:29

"For the gifts and calling of God are without repentance."

When you know God has called you, and given you a vision, rest assured God will cause that vision to be accomplished. God knows what He is doing. Regardless of your good or bad choices, He knew the things you would do before He formed you in the womb. The New International Version Bible says, *"For God's gifts and his call are irrevocable."* **(Romans 11:29).** God has not changed His mind!

Are you so prideful to think you have sinned greater than God has power to forgive? Do you think you are so wicked God cannot deliver you from torrents of turmoil, torment and emotional torture? Do not be presumptuous! No sin you have committed is greater than the cleansing, healing, and restoring power of the blood of Jesus.

Surprised by your ability to fail and unable to make yourself forget harsh words that cannot be retracted, a fit of rage, an abortion, a lost child, or an infidelity, you allow *unbelief* to hide behind these and other issues. The fallacy is that you caught God off guard when you made those choices. If you have repented for wrongdoing and turned again to God, He is faithful to forgive and will help you every step of the way. Be ever mindful though, you *must* repent.

Who better to reach an alcoholic than a saved and delivered alcoholic? Who better to steer a young girl away from pre-marital sex or prostitution than someone who has walked that path and been delivered? If you could see the way God intends to clean up and use these terrible, life-altering mistakes, you would be rejoicing right now. You *must* believe this! It is the pathway to your deliverance.

You do not need to wait for all of the changes to be complete before beginning to move into your destiny. God knows exactly where you have been and where you are, which is precisely why He is uniquely qualified to take you to your God-given destination. He is in control, and He has a plan to turn your mistakes around and use them for His purpose.

IDENTIFYING UNBELIEF

As previously stated, *unbelief* is sometimes difficult to identify. It hinders spirit-filled believers from moving ahead with the Lord and achieving their destiny and keeps non-believers from coming to a saving knowledge of Jesus Christ.

Do you have problem areas that will not come in line with what you know to be God's plan for you? Do you see *your* problems as mountains standing between you and where God is taking you? Do you have needs that remain unfulfilled, though you continually ask

God to supply? Speaking *of* the problems or needs is *NOT* your answer. Speaking *to* the mountain is the answer; the mountain called **UNBELIEF!**

It is crucial that you recognize the *problems* you are experiencing are *NOT* the mountain. You will create a mountain of *unbelief* with your mouth by speaking of the problems instead of the *Word of God.* Talking about trouble makes it seem more significant and powerful than it is in reality. Rehearsing problems causes a foreboding, dark, disaster-threatening cloud to loom over you. Negative talk is used by the devil to make you feel powerless and hopeless.

Your problems are only *foothills* at the base of a mountain of *unbelief.* As overwhelming as they seem when you stand next to them, they are small in comparison to the mountain of *unbelief* keeping these situations *in control.* **UNBELIEF** is the *root* of your problems; **UNBELIEF** is the *reason* why you do not see victory. When you deal with your mountain of *unbelief,* it starts a process whereby all other obstacles standing between you and your destiny will come into line. Deal with the mountain of *unbelief,* and this will bring the foothills you call problems into perspective!

ALL THINGS WORK TOGETHER FOR GOOD

Romans 8:28

"And we know that all things work together for good to them that love God, to them who are the called according to his purpose." **Romans 8:28.**

70   Faith as . . .

The Bible does not say some things work together, or a few things work together, but it says *"ALL things work together"*! Everything you have done or been God will use to bring about His purpose. God did not say only the good things work for good. He says *all* things work together for good. The good, the bad, and the ugly work together for your good because you love Him and are the *called* according to His purpose!

2 Corinthians 9:8

"And God is able to make all grace abound toward you; that ye, always having all sufficiency in all things, may abound to every good work:"

God is able to supply you with all you need for every good work. The Amplified Bible says it this way: *"And God is able to make all grace abound to you, so that in all things at all times, having all that you need, you will abound in every good work."* (2Corinthians 9:8) Look at the definition of *"grace"*. It is defined as *"unmerited divine assistance given humans for their regeneration or sanctification"*. The word *"abound"* means *"present in great quantity, fully or abundantly supplied"*. This scripture teaches that God is able to give you unmerited, divine assistance that will be present in great quantity to regenerate *(or form again)* and sanctify *(give moral sanction to)* you. This means, in *ALL* things at *ALL* times you will have *ALL* you need! You will be fully and abundantly supplied in *EVERY* good work. God is a wonderful God! No matter what you have done, where you have been, who others think you are or think you will never be, all of those things work together for your good. God is able to give you everything you need to succeed in what He has called you to do.

6

UNBELIEF, IT IS A MOUNTAIN

THE COMPOSITION OF MOUNTAINS

Natural mountains are composed of different elements and formed in different ways. Similarly, mountains of *unbelief* form by different problems, circumstances, and situations that arise in your life. Regardless of its make-up, *ALL* forms of the mountain of *unbelief* are detrimental to your goal of running the race and reaching your destination.

Man studies natural mountains to learn what is inside the earth and what forces shape it. A close look at the mountain of *unbelief* will tell you something about the forces shaping it and will reveal what is on the inside of you. Are you hard or soft and pliable? Are you barren or productive? Are you walking in *"faith as a grain of mustard seed"* or in "Plain, Old, Ordinary Faith"? Taking a closer look will help you to identify specific areas of *unbelief* and equip you to pray specifically and effectively.

As you deal with your mountain of *unbelief*, remember not to overlook the gems. Rich mineral deposits and precious gems can be gleaned as this mountain is moved. Hidden deep in natural mountains are precious gems coveted by all. Buried deep under the mountain of *unbelief* that has troubled your life, are beautiful gems waiting to be mined. Allow Jesus to take over the mining process. The issues which have caused pain and suffering in your life are like precious and valuable gems. As with natural gems, when mined, cut, polished, and placed in the proper setting, they become adorning pieces of jewelry for many to enjoy their beauty.

NO MOUNTAIN CLIMBING

God does not intend you to climb your mountain of *unbelief*. He wants it removed altogether. As you continue to travel in the direction of your destiny, you may feel it is uphill. If the journey gets more difficult and you are out of breath, realize you are climbing the mountain instead of removing it.

If you climb a natural mountain, you are likely to run into bad weather at some point. The same is true when you climb your mountain of *unbelief*. The higher you climb on a natural mountain, the colder the temperature gets. As warm air moves up the windward slope *(the side where the wind blows)*, it comes down as rain or snow.

How true this is in the spiritual realm. When you are moving in a direction contrary to what the Lord requires of you, a great deal of bad weather will come. You *must* walk in obedience. You can easily be blind-sided, by the devil, when you are disobedient to the Lord. Remember, the Lord instructed you to speak to your mountain of *unbelief, NOT* climb it.

Climbing a natural mountain during bad weather can be dangerous. You could be blinded by rain, lose your way, or fall into a deep crevice! If you climb your mountain of *unbelief* rather than remove it, you are *likely* to be blinded, lose your way, or fall down.

Suppose you *were* to make it to the top of the mountain, what would you find? According to the study of natural mountains, the far side is the *leeward* side. When air passes the crest of the mountain it becomes drier and causes a *"rain shadow"* on the other side. What does that mean? Many of the world's *deserts* lie in rain shadows. Think about it! You managed to keep your footing and climbed the mountain only to find a dry, barren desert on the other side.

Do you *still* want to climb your mountain of *unbelief*? How many times have you found yourself in a desert on the leeward side crying out to the Lord, *"Where are you?"* Your prayers are dry; your worship is flat; everything around you seems lifeless. Realize this one thing, *you* moved, not *God*. Yes, *YOU* left **Him** on the other side of the mountain. The Lord did not abandon you. If you are struggling with each step, stop and evaluate your position. Allow Jesus to lovingly *unveil* your *unbelief*. He is waiting for you to realize the futility of climbing the mountain of *unbelief*.

HOW MOUNTAINS ARE FORMED

Natural mountains do not form overnight. They form over long periods of time due to tremendous forces in the earth. Spiritually speaking, the mountain of *unbelief* in you may have been created over a long period by tremendous forces in *YOUR* earth. You do not look out over a plain one minute and see a mountain the next. Natural and spiritual mountains are formed gradually.

A theory called *plate tectonics* explains mountain formation. According to this theory, the earth's outer shell is made up of rigid plates of various sizes. These plates are in slow, continuous motion. Most mountain forming occurs along boundaries between plates. In the same way, a mountain of *unbelief* can occur between boundaries in your life. Everyone has places of stress or change when they are moving to another level. Life is in constant motion whether it appears to be or not. This continuous motion, with one situation moving against another, can create a mountain of *unbelief*.

There are five basic kinds of natural mountains, depending on the process by which they were formed. Though dealing with one mountain, the mountain of *unbelief*, it may form in a number of ways. You may not recognize your mountain of *unbelief* if you do not stop and notice how it was formed. Examine the following types of natural mountains and identify your mountain of *unbelief*.

VOLCANIC MOUNTAINS

The first type of mountain is volcanic. When molten rock from deep within the earth erupts and piles up on the surface, huge plates on the surface of the earth collide. The friction and heat cause the hot liquid rock to spew out from the center of the earth. After a while, this molten rock solidifies and forms a mountain.

Do you have a volcanic mountain of *unbelief* in you? Are there times that you erupt due to the friction and heat in your "earth"? When things boil under the surface for a long time, do you explode in anger? Attacks from the enemy may cause *"eruptions"* of anger and rage, especially if they are not dealt with through prayer and fasting. When you do not see deliverance, the pressure builds. If you do not exercise authority through Jesus Christ over problems, you may erupt. These eruptions build a mountain of *unbelief* within you.

Do not be in bondage to any of the things that cause a volcanic mountain of *unbelief!* Eruptions would not occur if you believed that *"all things work together for good"*. If you believed this, the lava of your life would not be spewing out on everyone passing by.

Believe God will use these situations to develop **"faith as a grain of mustard seed"** or faith that *"acts like"* a grain of mustard seed in you.

DOME MOUNTAINS

Dome Mountains are formed when forces under the surface of the earth lift the earth's crust into a broad bulge or dome. It may not be noticeable at first, but the area is vulnerable to increased erosion, which causes peaks and valleys to form.

In your life, the Dome Mountains may not show in the beginning. You may appear to have everything intact, but underneath there is damage. Over time, the pressures and problems begin to push up to the surface and erosion is the result. When erosion takes place, it affects your relationship with God and man. The peaks are high and the valleys are low and in between lie many jagged edges.

Since a dome mountain begins as a raised section and not a large looming mountain, it can go undetected for some time. A dome mountain of *unbelief* can manifest as health problems, emotional problems, or low self-esteem resulting in bad life choices. Perhaps you are a person who does not express yourself outwardly. You may be under constant stress from trouble in your personal life, family, or ministry. If these things continue, a dome mountain of *unbelief* may occur. This constant pressure with no outlet can make you feel hopeless and depressed.

Do not allow adversity to build a dome mountain of *unbelief.* Look to God to release the pressure and stop the erosion of your health, emotional stability, and well being. Allow God to use these circumstances to develop *"faith as a grain of mustard seed"* or faith that *"acts like"* a grain of mustard seed in you.

FAULT-BLOCK MOUNTAINS

Fault-Block Mountains are huge blocks of the earth's crust that tilt or push up along a fracture causing major shifts or breaks. *Rapid* erosion occurs and debris collects at the base of the mountain.

Do you have Fault-Block Mountains in you? When traumatic events happen that you cannot control, do major shifts or breaks occur?

These incidents, if not properly dealt with in prayer, become a mountain of *unbelief.*

If you allow your belief system to be affected by adverse events that occur, you may blame God for the unfavorable things that have happened to you. If you are not completely grounded and do not have a strong foundation in the *Word of God*, you will believe the lies of the devil. He will tell you God does not love you or He would not allow bad events to happen. The devil will attempt to convince you that God would protect you if you *really* belonged to him. After a period of time, you may lose hope that God cares for you or is aware of your needs. You are believing lies from the enemy.

The key is to recognize that God *is* aware of every adverse experience you go through and can turn unfavorable events into something favorable. The *occurrences* that form a Fault-Block Mountain of *unbelief* can become *experiences* that will enable you to minister to others. You cannot change what has happened, but you can give *all* unfortunate situations to God. Allow Him to use them to develop **"faith as a grain of mustard seed"** or faith that *"acts like"* a grain of mustard seed by which you can remove the mountain of *unbelief.*

EROSION MOUNTAINS

Erosion Mountains result from the erosion of a thick pile of sedimentary rock. Rivers and glaciers erode a large area of sedimentary rock to form peaks and valleys.

An erosion mountain of *unbelief* is formed when everyday problems slowly erode the structure of your life. These are not necessarily major breaks, but little things here and there. Your foundation is strong, but the combination of many little incidents form a constant stream used by the enemy to draw your focus away from your destiny. The devil uses a constant influx of *little* issues to distract you and convince you that you will never reach the destiny God has promised. The devil uses these to wear you out and wear you down.

Allow the Lord to fill in the gaps left by this erosion and allow Him to remove the little things that erode your life. He will use the peaks and valleys to develop ***"faith as a grain of mustard seed"*** or faith that *"acts like"* a grain of mustard seed in you and remove the erosion mountain of *unbelief.*

FOLD MOUNTAINS

The earth's plates have thick deposits of sedimentary (*layered*) rock around the edges, and these plates will sometimes hit head on. When they do, they push each other back and up. This back-and-up motion makes wrinkles in the earth. These natural mountains are called Fold Mountains.

Spiritually speaking, it is possible to have Fold Mountains of *unbelief,* also. Have you ever seen two Christians collide head-on in disagreement? It is possible for people to be working side by side with God's Kingdom as their common goal and disagree so strongly that it adversely affects both. This also has the potential to affect others.

A common misconception is that believers will always agree. This is simply not true. God made each of us individuals, and there will be disagreements. People rarely recognize that the result of these disagreements can be a mountain of *unbelief.* When feelings are hurt, or disagreements arise, people tend to lose sight of the big picture. No matter who is responsible, butting up against one another can lead to the formation of a mountain of *unbelief.* This may cause everyone involved to be delayed in reaching their destiny.

MOUNTAINS AT A DISTANCE

Natural mountains are formed over a period of many years by a variety of changes in the environment. When these changes occur together and frequently enough, mountain *ranges* are formed. These mountain ranges sometimes form dividing walls or barriers.

Spiritually speaking, this happens when you allow *unbelief* to remain in you. It begins to form a mountain or range of mountains that serve as a barrier between you and your destiny. You are on your way to a destiny ordained by God, but a mountain looms in front of you. This mountain, or range of mountains, can be large enough and high enough to keep you from finishing your course.

God gives revelation through His word to help you locate the mountain of *unbelief.* Sometimes people are sent to enlighten you. Have you ever received correction from a brother or sister in Christ? This can be a difficult thing to accept when done in love, *but* you *may* be corrected by a person with a wrong motive in an inappropriate way. When this happens, do not reject the correction automatically. It can work for your good. Instead of being offended by their wrong motives or approach and allowing it to cause you to have a wrong spirit, pray and ask God to reveal anything in you that coincides with what they are saying. Maybe they are right about your need for correction and if you refuse to develop a bitter or resentful spirit toward them, you will benefit from the situation. If you realize people are imperfect vessels being used by the God who loves you, then you can receive and grow from the correction. Failure to do so creates another barrier between you and your destiny.

Natural mountains have long served as barriers. They have hindered transportation, settlement, and communication. The isolation of people living in the mountains has created much diversity in cultures. For example, in Switzerland's Alps, people speak hundreds of dialects of four different languages.

This may be similar to denominational differences. There are many different denominations with different ideas about what is important in the *Kingdom of God*.

How many times has the mountain of *unbelief* served as a barrier between you and another person? How many times has communication between you and another brother or sister broken down due to differences? Have you ever felt like the Christians surrounding you are all going in different directions and speaking different languages? How many times are you hindered due to the barriers formed by the mountain of *unbelief*?

MOUNTAINS AS VACATION SPOTS

Natural mountains are also used as recreational areas. Millions of people travel to the mountains to enjoy the view and to engage in such activities as camping, hiking, skiing, and snow boarding. Have you climbed part of the way up your mountain of *unbelief* and decided to camp there? Is the mountain of *unbelief* the hottest vacation spot this year? Is it so popular with everyone that there are no vacancies? The mountain that *now* appears to be a nice vacation spot will eventually become a death trap to you and others. Do not get comfortable on this mountain and linger there to enjoy the view! As long as you are *"camped out"*, you will never reach your destination. Do not climb this mountain, *MOVE IT!*

REMOVAL IS YOUR ONLY OPTION

Face it. You absolutely must, *REMOVE* this mountain of *unbelief* from your life. The Lord does not want you to travel *"over"* or *"around"* the mountain, and He does not want you to move it shovel by shovel. The Lord wants you to *speak* to the mountain and remove it. Things are so much easier when you do them *His* way! How unnecessarily tired you make yourself when you do things *your* way. The Lord's instructions are simple: exercise your ***"faith as a grain of mustard seed"***; speak to the mountain; *REMOVE* it; and *nothing shall be impossible unto you.*

As you pray in the Spirit, study, and speak the *Word of God*, you create a new mountain in your life-*A MOUNTAIN OF FAITH!*

Faith as . . .

7

UNBELIEF AND JESUS' MINISTRY TEAM

UNBELIEF ACCORDING TO JESUS

Matthew 17: 20

"And Jesus rebuked the devil; and he departed out of him: and the child was cured from that very hour. Then came the disciples to Jesus apart, and said, Why could not we cast him out? And Jesus said unto them, Because of your unbelief: for verily I say unto you, If ye have faith as a grain of mustard seed, ye shall say unto this mountain, Remove hence to yonder place; and it shall remove; and nothing shall be impossible unto you."

Let us look at *unbelief* from Jesus' point of view. This is where you must look if you are to understand what is holding you back from your destiny. The disciples could not understand why they were unable to cast the demon out of the young man. Jesus had no problem delivering him. Unlike His disciples, He was not dealing with a mountain. Jesus told them plainly their *unbelief* was the problem. He said, *"Because of your unbelief . . ."*

Imagine how confusing it must have been to the disciples for Jesus to make that statement. These men were His chosen disciples. They were believers. They had seen many miracles, how could they be in *unbelief*? As always, though, Jesus lovingly took the time to explain what He meant so that they could understand. He said, *"If you have faith as a grain of mustard seed you can say unto this mountain remove hence to yonder place; and it shall remove; and nothing shall be impossible unto you"*.

Jesus does not play games. If you ask Him a question, He gives you a straight answer. Jesus never talks like *super spiritual* people who use *hundred dollar words for explanation* when they only have *a dime's worth of revelation*! When Jesus talks, you never go away with more questions than when you started. If you ask Him a question, He gives you a simple, straight answer.

The answer Jesus gave the disciples was that they had a mountain that needed removing. Yes, they were standing at the foot of a *literal* mountain, but that was not the mountain to which Jesus referred. He was addressing a specific mountain *within* His disciples, the mountain of *unbelief*! What some would see as the mountain of *illness* in the young man was moved. Jesus rebuked the devil and it had left him. Jesus was not reaching back to something already finished.

86   *Faith as . . .*

He was addressing why His disciples could not cast the demon out before He came on the scene.

The question was *"Why could not we cast him out?"* The answer was simple. There was a mountain in them, a mountain of *unbelief!* A huge obstruction stood between the power given to these men earlier and the young man's need. What is puzzling about this is, Jesus had given the disciples *POWER* and *AUTHORITY* over *ALL* devils, *AND* to cure disease!

POWER AND AUTHORITY

Luke 9:1-2

"Then he called his twelve disciples together, and gave them power and authority over all devils, and to cure diseases. And he sent them to preach the kingdom of God, and to heal the sick."

It is important to note this passage in **Luke 9** before we progress further. Luke explains that Jesus called the disciples together and gave them power and authority over all devils and to cure diseases. He then sent them out to exercise that power and authority. Nevertheless, the disciples found themselves powerless while dealing with the demon in this young man.

Was the demonic influence in the young man's life beyond the scope of power Jesus had given His disciples? Did Jesus say they had authority over *some* devils but not others? Did He say, "the *little* devils you can handle, but those big, strong, long lasting devils, you had better leave up to me? *NO!* He gave them power and authority over *ALL* devils, *AND* to cure diseases!

You do not know how much time has lapsed between these events, but it is significant that they are recorded in the same chapter. On the heels of Jesus' disciples receiving all power and authority, comes the opportunity to exercise it. Not only could the disciples *NOT* cast the demon out of the young man, they also had to *ASK why* they could not. How quickly they had forgotten.

How quickly you and I forget. We go to revival, hear our prophecy, and shout *"Amen!"* Then, go away only to forget what was said, or worse yet, we give in to discouragement the minute the devil comes against us.

ALL TWELVE disciples had everything they needed to cast out this demon. How faithful God is to equip you and immediately give you opportunity to test your new authority. This was a small test-one young man, one demon. The demon controlling this young man, however, was skilled at destruction and in command of his life. That is not to be taken lightly. This demon was comfortable, and did not intend to leave. This demon knew it had control of the situation because it recognized the mountain of *unbelief* in the disciples.

Jesus was only apart from them for a short time. When He returned, He found His disciples had all but forgotten the assignments of the past few weeks. They had been given power and authority over *ALL* devils, power, and authority to cure *ALL* diseases, but they could not cure one young man. What is up with this? Jesus' disciples had seen first-hand the miracles He had performed. He healed the sick, caused the blind to see, the deaf to hear, and raised the dead. They had been given that *same* power and authority. Now, the disciples had come face-to-face with one determined demon in one young man, and they were defeated!

Think about this! These were Jesus' disciples, they had experienced the manifestation of the power of God. What could prevent them from exercising their faith and seeing this young man delivered? *A MOUNTAIN!* Jesus said a *mountain* was the reason the disciples could not cure the young man. They had a mountain of *UNBELIEF* and it had grown to such a height it hindered them from doing what God had *fully* equipped them to do. The disciples knew *Jesus* could deliver the boy, but their *veiled* mountain of *unbelief* kept them from realizing they had authority to do the same thing Jesus did!

This is true of many people. God has given all power and authority to you through Jesus' Name, but still nothing happens. You do not see manifestations of the power of God because there is a mountain of *unbelief* in you that needs removed before you can fulfill your *God-given destiny*.

UNBELIEF UNDERMINES VICTORY

Unbelief is a strong spirit. The devil builds a mountain of *unbelief* in you by deception. You assume because you gain some victory that *unbelief* is not present. A certain amount of victory comes with any level of faith, but this is not the same as living victoriously with *"faith as a grain of mustard seed"* or faith that *"acts like"* a grain of mustard seed".

Unbelief is so misleading it affected the ministry team of Jesus. The men who walked the earth beside the Son of God struggled with *unbelief* and were unaware of it. Jesus' disciples were unable to experience power and deliverance in the ministry though they had authority. When Jesus addressed the problem, He said it was because of their *unbelief.* That was it! *UNBELIEF* was *THE* problem! It was nothing *except THEIR UNBELIEF*!

Matthew, Mark, and Luke all give an account of the demon-possessed boy and the father who came to Jesus' disciples for deliverance for his son. Each account has important details worth reviewing.

Matthew 17:14-20

"And when they were come to the multitude, there came to him a certain man, kneeling down to him, and saying, Lord, have mercy on my son: for he is lunatic, and sore vexed: for ofttimes he falleth into the fire, and oft into the water. And I brought him to thy disciples, and they could not cure him. Then Jesus answered and said, O faithless and perverse generation, how long shall I be with you? how long shall I suffer you? bring him hither to me. And Jesus rebuked the devil; and he departed out of him: and the child was cured from that very hour. Then came the disciples to Jesus apart, and said, Why could not we cast him out? And Jesus said unto them, Because of your unbelief: for verily I say unto you, If ye have faith as a grain of mustard seed, ye shall say unto this mountain, Remove hence to

*yonder place; and it shall remove; and nothing shall
be impossible unto you."*

In Matthew's account, the man kneels before Jesus and asks
for mercy for his son. He had brought the boy to the disciples, and
they could not cure him. After hearing what had happened, Jesus
replied, *"Oh faithless and perverse generation, how long shall I be
with you and how long shall I suffer you, bring him hither to me".*
Why do you think Jesus said this? One man and his son had a
problem, but Jesus was addressing *all* of the people nearby. The Bible
says there was a *"multitude"* that came. Was there not enough *"faith"*
in the multitude of people and disciples to deliver the young man? Oh,
untrusting, unbelieving, and corrupt people, Jesus was saying, how
long must I suffer you? How long must I bear you up before you
finally catch on? The reason I am here is to show you the way. How
long shall I endure? How long shall I experience your unfaithful,
unbelieving hearts? *"Bring him hither to Me",* Jesus said. He
rebuked the devil and the devil departed.

After Jesus rebuked the devil, the child was cured from that
very hour. He was delivered in sixty minutes or less! There is a cry to
God for some sixty-minute or less miracles! God's people need some
sixty-minute or less miracles! They need some sixty-minute or less
answers to their prayers! The Bible says, *"The child was cured from
that very hour".*

After seeing how quickly the demon went from the boy, Jesus'
disciples were probably a bit embarrassed or confused. They went to
Jesus apart (*away from the crowd of people*) and said, *"Why could we*

not cast him out?" They could not cast out the devil because *unbelief* was *veiled* in their hearts.

Mark 9:14-29

"And straightway all the people, when they beheld him, were greatly amazed, and running to him saluted him. And he asked the scribes, What question ye with them? And one of the multitude answered and said, Master, I have brought unto thee my son, which hath a dumb spirit; And wheresoever he taketh him, he teareth him: and he foameth, and gnasheth with his teeth, and pineth away: and I spake to thy disciples that they should cast him out; and they could not. He answereth him, and saith, O faithless generation, how long shall I be with you? how long shall I suffer you? bring him unto me. And they brought him unto him: and when he saw him, straightway the spirit tare him; and he fell on the ground, and wallowed foaming. And he asked his father, How long is it ago since this came unto him? And he said, Of a child. And ofttimes it hath cast him into the fire, and into the waters, to destroy him: but if thou canst do any thing, have compassion on us, and help us. Jesus said unto him, If thou canst believe, all things are possible to him that believeth. And straightway the father of the child cried out, and said with tears, Lord, I believe; help thou mine unbelief. When Jesus saw that the people came running together, he rebuked the foul spirit, saying unto him, Thou dumb and deaf spirit, I charge thee, come out of him, and enter no more into him. And the spirit cried, and rent him sore, and came out of him: and he was as one dead; insomuch that many said, He is dead. But Jesus took him by the hand, and lifted him up; and he arose. And when he was come into the house, his disciples asked him

*privately, Why could not we cast him out? And he
said unto them, This kind can come forth by nothing,
but by prayer and fasting. And they departed thence,
and passed through Galilee; and he would not that
any man should know it. For he taught his disciples,
and said unto them, The Son of man is delivered into
the hands of men, and they shall kill him; and after
that he is killed, he shall rise the third day. But they
understood not that saying, and were afraid to ask
him. And he came to Capernaum: and being in the
house he asked them, What was it that ye disputed
among yourselves by the way? But they held their
peace: for by the way they had disputed among
themselves, who should be the greatest."*

In Mark's account, you see Jesus asked this father how long
this had been happening to his son. The man said it had been
happening since he was a child. This demon had been with this young
man ALL of his life. All of his life the young man had been dealing
with this problem. All of his life he had been thrown down, beaten up,
and torn apart by the spirit that would not leave him. How he must
have longed for deliverance! How his father must have longed for
deliverance! You can imagine both father and son must have
awakened each morning hoping this day would be different. Maybe
today he would be *"normal"*. Maybe today deliverance would come.
Maybe today. . .

Some have been dealing with a problem for many years. It
might be your personal life, ministry, marriage, or family. Whatever
the area, the devil has latched on, and you have been dealing with it for
a *long* time. You have looked at this problem for so long it seems

impossible to rid yourself of it. How many times have you tried to overcome it? How many times have you tried to start again, on a new day, only to find yourself thrown down and torn apart one more time? How many times have you repeated a behavior or fallen back into a pattern no matter how determined you were that *today* would be different?

The world calls this cycling, but the root of the problem is *unbelief.* This cycle has been a part of you so long you do not *believe* it can be broken. You have prayed for deliverance, but each time you find yourself back at square one, in yet another prayer line, or in your prayer closet again dealing with this same problem. One minute you are laying hands on someone, the power of God manifests, and they receive instant healing and deliverance. The next minute you are facing defeat in *your* situations.

It does not matter who you are or where you come from. You may be the best-dressed, wealthiest, most poised person. You might be a pastor, elder, deacon, laymen, prayer coordinator, etc. No matter what your background, you can identify. Each of you struggles with at least one *thing* you have struggled with for a long time. You have cried and tried, but there seems to be no possible way to gain victory in this *one* area. Your life could be victorious in ministry, marriage, and money – if it were not for this *one thing*.

The root problem is *UNBELIEF!* *Unbelief* is a tool of the devil. He uses it to hinder you because it is difficult to identify. When experiencing miracles and victory for others, *unbelief* may be *veiled* in you. You cannot allow this to happen. Ask God to illuminate the darkness and reveal *veiled* areas of *unbelief.* God is faithful to show you those areas and enables you to remove them.

HELP THOU MY UNBELIEF
Mark 9:21-23

" And he asked his father, How long is it ago since this came unto him? And he said, Of a child. And ofttimes it hath cast him into the fire, and into the waters, to destroy him: but if thou canst do any thing, have compassion on us, and help us. Jesus said unto him, If thou canst believe, all things are possible to him that believeth."

Jesus said *"if"* you can believe, all things are possible. Why did he say "if"? Remember, this father had watched his son suffer all his life. Jesus heard the father say, *"If" thou canst do anything"*. Jesus detected a thread of *unbelief* in this father's tapestry of faith. There was a big, beautiful woven picture of *"He can do this, He has done it for others", "He has such compassion"* and *"the last person was healed instantly,"* but there was a thread of *unbelief.* Jesus had to deal with that *unbelief* before the son could receive deliverance.

The father came to Jesus believing, but one little *"if"* woven into the picture was enough to keep his son from deliverance. One little thread of doubt was enough to jeopardize the miracle. One little *"maybe there is nothing anyone can do"*, one little, *"why would He do it for me"*, one little *"but, my son has been this way for so long"* could have kept this young man in bondage for the rest of his life.

The father had hope. He was there to get his son cured. In the beginning, he may have thought, *"my son will grow out of this"* or *"we will find a good physician to cure him"*, but years passed and nothing materialized. Then he heard about Jesus and His disciples and the miracles surrounding their ministry. Surely, *they* could cure his son!

The father started out strong, but his son had suffered so many years. After all this time, all of the suffering, all of the dashed hopes, *unbelief* had formed a mountain. When Jesus' disciples could not cure his son, the father began to waiver. After everything he had been through, the father allowed compromise to enter into his thinking.

One definition of compromise is *"to find or follow a way between extremes"*. Another way to define compromise is *"something intermediate between or blending qualities of two different things"*. The father had been so disappointed for such a long time; he was willing to settle for *"something in between"*. Originally, he wanted his son completely cured, but by the time the father had reached Jesus, he was asking, ***"if thou canst do ANYTHING, have compassion on us, and help us"***.

For this desperate father, *anything* Jesus could do would have been enough, but Jesus saw the compromise in the father and spoke straight forwardly to him. ***"If thou canst believe, all things are possible to him that believeth"***. Jesus wanted the father to know he had come to the right place. Not only could He cure his son, but He could do much more. With Jesus, *ALL* things are possible. Not only did his son not have to suffer anymore, but also anything the father

needed in any area of life was available! If only he could believe!
What a revelation!

Mark 9:24

*"And straightway the father of the child cried out,
and said with tears, Lord, I believe; help thou mine
unbelief!"*

At that moment, the father understood. By divine revelation,
he knew *unbelief* would hinder; *unbelief* would destroy; *unbelief* would
stop his son's healing yet another time. It dawned on this father that
his unbelief would cause his *son* to continue to struggle with this
demon indefinitely.

The father's cry was, *"Lord, I believe, help thou mine
unbelief"*! The father had suffered along with his son. They had tried
every avenue, every physician, every medicinal cure, *EVERYTHING!*
The father had a desire to see his son healed, but he had to *believe* it
would happen. The father thought he believed. He thought he had
faith, but through the words of Jesus, the father realized he had allowed
unbelief to creep in. The father recognized Jesus was *unveiling*
something in him he was not aware was there. This father knew
everything was contingent upon this statement from Jesus. He knew
that for his son, this was the last chance. This spirit was in complete
control of his only son. This moment would determine whether his
only son would die at the hands of the demon controlling him or live in
total deliverance. He *must* understand what Jesus was saying in order
for his son to experience deliverance.

HANGING ON TO EVERY WORD

This father was so desperate for a miracle he received the revelation for his need *before* Jesus' ministry team did! He was desperately hanging on *every word* the Lord Jesus spoke to him. God is looking for those who will *"hang"* on His *every* Word, whether it comes forth from the pulpit, the prayer closet, or through the prophets. Sometimes people have to be desperate before God can perform miracles in their lives. People, like the disciples who were directly involved in the ministry, may get a little too confident. If you are not careful, you find yourself around anointed people and become somewhat desensitized to the anointing. You may hang around the church, soaking up the Word and start to think *you* have all of the answers. It is easy to get a little cocky when everything is going well.

Remember though, the father was not with the *"in"* crowd. He was not accustomed to *"hanging out"* with anointed people. He was not *"hanging out"* acting spiritual. He was *"hanging out"* with a sick child. His life consisted of daily watching his son suffer. He hung on to the life of his son, while a demon was hanging on just as strongly. The father knew *he* did not have all the answers. The one thing this father *did* know was that he was a desperate man in need of a miracle.

This father must have been thinking, *"Lord, I do believe. That is why I came. I brought my son to your ministry team. I do believe, but maybe I have allowed unbelief to creep in."* **Lord, I believe; help thou my unbelief".** That is revelation knowledge from God! *Unbelief Unveiled!*

A TEACHING EXERCISE

Mark 9:2a

"And after six days Jesus taketh with him Peter, and James, and John, and leadeth them up into an high mountain apart by themselves:"

Jesus had taken only a few of His disciples up on the mount with Him. He did this for more than one reason. The fact that He left some of them at the bottom with the people gave those disciples an opportunity to exercise what they had been taught. To give them head-knowledge was good, but what they had learned would have to be tested. They would have to reach deep down and pull out the root of what they had been taught. They needed to take a good hard look at the situation and realize they truly had been given power to perform miracles, *too*. No matter who was wagging their tongue, shaking their heads, laughing, or ridiculing them, they had power. Jesus had given them *all* they needed.

Luke 9:36-43a

"And when the voice was past, Jesus was found alone. And they kept it close, and told no man in those days any of those things which they had seen. And it came to pass, that on the next day, when they were come down from the hill, much people met him. And, behold, a man of the company cried out, saying, Master, I beseech thee, look upon my son: for he is mine only child. And, lo, a spirit taketh him, and he suddenly crieth out; and it teareth him that he foameth again, and bruising him hardly departeth from him. And I besought thy disciples to cast him out; and they could not. And Jesus answering said,

O faithless and perverse generation, how long shall I be with you, and suffer you? Bring thy son hither. And as he was yet a coming, the devil threw him down, and tare him. And Jesus rebuked the unclean spirit, and healed the child, and delivered him again to his father. And they were all amazed at the mighty power of God."

Luke tells us that the father brought his only son. He brought him to Jesus' disciples, *(the nine left at the bottom of the mountain)* and they could not cure him. They *COULD NOT!* Therefore the man approaches Jesus and cries, *"Master, I beseech you"* or I am begging you, *look upon my son because this is my only child and a spirit has control of him and suddenly he cries out. It throws him down, he gets bruised, and it never seems to leave him alone. I requested earnestly that your disciples cast him out; and they could not. **THEY COULD NOT!***

The Bible says Jesus answered and said, *"Oh, faithless and perverse generation, how long shall I be with you? How long shall I suffer you? Bring him to me."*

While the young man was coming, the spirit threw him down. There, in the presence of Jesus, the devil was torturing this young man! Jesus rebuked the devil; the devil left; and the young man was presented to his father. All the people were amazed at the power of God, but while the crowd marveled, Jesus had something important to say to His disciples.

LET IT SINK IN

Luke 9:43b-48

"But while they wondered every one at all things which Jesus did, he said unto his disciples, let these sayings sink down into your ears: for the Son of man shall be delivered into the hands of men. But they understood not this saying, and it was hid from them, that they perceived it not: and they feared to ask him of that saying. Then there arose a reasoning among them, which of them should be the greatest. And Jesus, perceiving the thought of their heart, took a child, and set him by him, And said unto them, Whosoever shall receive this child in my name receiveth me; and whosoever shall receive me receiveth him that sent me: for he that is least among you all, the same shall be great".

A teacher sometimes draws attention to a specific point in a lesson because it is a key concept. Jesus did this with His disciples. He wanted them to pay close attention. They desperately needed to learn this lesson on *unbelief.* Jesus knew if they did not grasp this key, they would not fully develop their faith. He was aware of what lay ahead for the disciples: rejection, hardships, persecutions, etc. He knew they would have to develop *"faith as a grain of mustard seed"* or faith that *"acts like"* a grain of mustard seed in order to continue steadfast in the faith.

Jesus realized He had little time left; He and the disciples would not be together much longer. Jesus encouraged His disciples to *"Let these sayings sink down into their ears".* The Bible says they did not understand what He meant; it was hid from them. In the midst of the celebration over the miracle of the young man's deliverance, Jesus had a golden nugget of knowledge for the disciples, but *they missed it.* They were afraid to ask Jesus what He meant. They were afraid to go to Him and say, *"Jesus, I simply do not understand; reveal to me what I am missing. Help me with my unbelief!"* They were content to reason things out in their minds, instead of allowing Jesus to enlighten them. Maybe the disciples did not want to appear ignorant. Confusion and embarrassment over not being able to cast the demon out of the young man may have been why they were afraid to ask Jesus to explain what He meant by this saying.

The devil came and distracted the disciples though, and their fleshly minds quickly came into agreement with him. They moved on to something they could perceive--*who would be the greatest among them!* Now, *this* was a topic they felt they could discuss intelligently!

This happens when pride enters and you do not humble yourself before the Lord. Keep your focus and make an effort to understand what the Lord is saying. When you have a question, simply ask Him for the answer. Do not be afraid to ask the Lord to reveal something you do not understand.

If you are confused about *anything* you read in the Bible, pray and ask the Lord for clarity. The Bible tells us in **1 Corinthians 14:33a *"God is not the author of confusion"*.** If you do not stop and ask questions, you rob yourself of an opportunity to bond with your Lord and Savior, Jesus Christ. Do not let fear or pride keep you from expressing to the Lord your lack of understanding and your need for help. The Lord longs to make His Word alive to you. He longs to communicate with you. *BELIEVE* and give Him a chance!

8

DESTINY DELAYED –
THE DEVIL'S DELIGHT

DEVIL, DO NOT ENTER

Have you ever allowed the devil to steal the *Word of God* from your heart? How many times have you received a Word from the Lord and before you got outside the church, you faced discouragement? You receive a Word for financial blessing and the car breaks down in the parking lot. Your Word was for health and while shaking the pastor's hand at the back door, you are attacked with major pain in your body. The devil uses situations to cause you to question what God has spoken to you.

John 10:10
"The thief cometh not, but for to steal, and to kill, and to destroy. . ."

The devil does come; you can expect it. The Bible does not say that Christians are exempt from the attacks of the enemy. The devil is diligent in his work. He is always seeking an opportunity to knock you off your feet. He is always seeking an opportunity to come against the fresh new Word you have heard from God. The thief comes immediately to steal the *Word of God* from you. Be on alert at all times! Recognize and deal with *unbelief.* Develop the *"faith as a grain of mustard seed"* or faith that *"acts like"* a grain of mustard seed necessary for you to defeat the devil and finish your race.

What is Satan using to attack you? How is he bringing *unbelief* into your life? This is an important question because *unbelief* cripples. It cripples families, friendships, marriage relationships, and ministries.

Sometimes it seems as though you are barely able to hold on to your vision. You love the Lord Jesus with all your heart, and your greatest desire is to accomplish *all* He has for you, but discouragement comes. You wake up some mornings not knowing how you will make it through the day. It seems as though the attacks never stop and although you attempt to remain focused and faithful, you are battle weary and struggle to continue. Choose to *glance* at your problems and *gaze* at your promise.

The devil is cruel, and he will come at you through any avenue accessible to him. Flesh and blood can be used to bring situations and circumstances that form a mountain of *unbelief*. The devil's desire is to cause you to stumble. He wants you to be delayed in reaching your destiny. If it means using others, he will.

Harboring offenses will delay your destiny. Someone may have said you were not good enough, would not follow through, did not come from the right background, or are not the right race or gender. You must not allow offense to form a mountain of *unbelief*.

If you allow your past to continually bring guilt and shame to your mind, your destiny will be delayed. Habitual sin controlling your life will delay your destiny. These things combined, creates a rubbish pile of wrong thinking that takes the form of a mountain of *unbelief*.

Each of us has a purpose, and this purpose has not been fulfilled. You cannot quit now. You *must* continue no matter how difficult things seem. As long as you are here, God is working in you to fulfill His purpose in the earth. Yes, the devil *has* tried to kill you, and if he could have, he would have. If he could stop you from moving into your destiny, he would. If he could get you to give up and quit, he would. If he could destroy every work in you that God has set in motion, he would do that, too. That is *his purpose*. Satan is a thief. He comes to *steal* the joy of your journey, *kill* any hope that you will finish the race, and *destroy* the weight of any godly influence you carry. Delaying your destiny is the devil's delight.

Satan knows that ultimately he cannot *stop* your destiny. He has *no* control over where you are going and cannot stop you from reaching your destination as it is God who is taking you there. Remember though, if he can *talk* you into a detour, *convince* you to be offended, or *entice* you to sin, he can build a mountain of *unbelief* and ultimately *DELAY* your destiny. He will do everything within his power to wear you out and wear you down. If you allow it, he will stop you in your tracks, but *you* are the *only* one who can actually stop yourself from reaching your destiny. You are the one who chooses to quit and never arrive at God's destination for you. If you do that, you will delight the devil. Surely, you would rather finish the race and delight the Lord!

It is sometimes difficult, as a Christian, to admit when you start to lose ground. You can easily begin to rely on your strength and not rely on the Holy Spirit for strength and guidance. When you do this, you are more vulnerable to the attacks of Satan. Pay close attention to your spiritual condition and always be on the lookout for the formation of a mountain of *unbelief.*

You can choose to turn away from your destiny, but if you are determined to walk with God and follow through, the devil can do nothing about it. The devil would like to remove you from service, take you out with illness, ruin you financially, take your children to hell, cause you to give up on God or kill your physical body; but I have good news for you! Allow God to develop *"faith as a grain of mustard seed"* or faith that *"acts like"* a grain of mustard seed and, the devil will not be able to do any of these things. Understand that there is no point at which you can turn your back on the devil and expect he will not attack. Be vigilant! *WATCH* and *PRAY!*

I Peter 5:8

"Be sober, be vigilant; because your adversary the devil, as a roaring lion, walketh about, seeking whom he may devour."

Pay close attention to these words sober and vigilant. To be sober is *to have an earnestly thoughtful character or demeanor. It is to be unhurried and calm, marked by temperance, moderation, or seriousness, and showing no excessive or extreme qualities of fancy, emotion, or prejudice.* To be vigilant is *to be especially watchful to avoid danger.* God is exhorting you to wake up and pay attention. The devil is looking for someone he *MAY* devour. May he devour *you*? *NO!* He may *try* to devour your thought life, your health, or your finances, but *you* have power to rebuke him. He may *try* to devour your entire belief system; but as you submit yourself to God and *"resist him he will flee from you"* according to **James 4:7**.

DESIRE DESTINY

Do not allow the devil to devour or steal anything God has promised you. You have the power needed to do the work God has given you to do.

You need to know, if God said it, He will do it! God is faithful, and He will see to it that you have all you need and you are able to do all He wants you to do, in spite of the circumstances surrounding you. As long as you desire to follow God and reach your destiny, God will see you through.

2 Chronicles 16:9a

"the eyes of the Lord run to and fro throughout the whole earth, to show himself strong in the behalf of them whose heart is perfect toward him."

The eyes of the Lord are running *"to and fro throughout the whole earth"*. Will He find in you one who desires to reach their destiny? Will He find in you one who will stop at nothing to receive the promise He has given? God is ready and waiting to help, but you must allow Him the opportunity to *"show himself strong"* on your behalf. God can help you learn a lesson from situations the devil uses to cause you to fail. When God is involved, circumstances turn around. What the devil sends to destroy your life and ministry can be the very thing God will use to propel you into your destiny. Simply ask the Lord to teach you through each situation. Ask God to reveal what is truth and what is not. If you do something bad, it does not mean you are bad. If someone else thinks you can or cannot accomplish a thing, it does not mean you can or cannot do it. If a person makes an accusation against you, it does not mean that is how or who you are. The mistakes you make or the opinions of others do not define you. **Colossians 3:3** says, *"For ye are dead and your life is hid with Christ in God."* The determining factor of who you are is who God says you are. Do not allow the devil to steal that from you.

9

THE CONSEQUENCES OF UNBELIEF

NO REST FOR THE REST

Hebrews 3: 18-19

"And to whom sware he that they should not enter into His rest, but to them that believed not? So we see that they could not enter in because of unbelief."

As you read **Hebrews 3: 18-19**, you will see the children of Israel could not enter into the Promised Land. You may have heard that the children of Israel could not enter because they murmured and complained. Maybe you thought they could not enter because they looked back to slavery, or they could not enter because they were having problems among themselves. This was not all-together true. It was not because they were tired of the food, could not find water or needed new clothes. It was not because they complained endlessly and wound up in idolatry. These problems were simply manifestations of a larger problem. The reason they could not enter in: their *unbelief.* *Unbelief* kept three to six million people out of the Promised Land! The ultimate reason they were unable to reach their destiny was *UNBELIEF!* If *unbelief* can keep God's chosen people from entering into what He promised them, *all* should take heed.

This should reveal to you that although it *looks* as if God is not able to deliver you, the root of your problem is *UNBELIEF.* No matter what circumstances arise and appear to be hindering your progress, no matter what situations arise that seem to be snuffing out your vision, the root may simply be *UNBELIEF.* You may not experience growth in your ministry, or deliverance for your family because of *UNBELIEF.* You may be hindered from entering into *your* Promised Land because of *UNBELIEF.*

AN ELEVEN-DAY JOURNEY

Remember, some of the Israelites were *born* in slavery. They had never known anything else. If you think a lifetime of slavery will not build a mountain of *unbelief, think again!* These people had grown so comfortable in their slavery they lost sight of their condition. They were miserable. Strangely enough, they were comfortable in their misery, so it was difficult for them to make a change and live outside of bondage. Everything about freedom was unknown and uncertain, and they complained as God began to bring about their deliverance.

The children of Israel had not developed *"faith as a grain of mustard seed"* or faith that *"acts like"* a grain of mustard seed during the time of their slavery. They had come to depend on taskmasters to tell them what to do and when to do it. They were fed, and had shelter.

The same thing happens today. How many people do you know who are comfortable in their slavery, seeing *bondage* as *'the good life'*? A family can be in bondage to demonic spirits and not realize it. Were you born into a *Christian* family that accepts anger, bitterness, resentment, poverty, sickness, depression, alcoholism, drug addictions, emotional dependence or other problems as a part of daily life? If this is the case, you may not realize you are in bondage because this life-style seems *"normal"* to you. When someone comes along and shows you a better way, you may resist the change they present. If so, you have become *comfortable* in your slavery. Be willing to be led out of bondage, trek through the wilderness, and occupy the Promised Land.

In order to maintain your freedom, develop *"faith as a grain of mustard seed"* or faith that *"acts like"* a grain of mustard seed. Without this kind of faith, freedom may not be attractive to you. The children of Israel were free, but they faced rough terrain and times of testing before they arrived at their Promised Land. Press in, check for a mountain of *unbelief* in your path and move it before the enemy of your soul entices you to turn around and go back into slavery. *Do not* go back into bondage. Maintain your freedom and the generations that follow will live free, also. Your example will demonstrate freedom as the *normal* way of life.

Note that the Promised Land was already deeded over to the children of Israel. It was theirs. All they had to do was accept the promise God had provided for them and make the trip. These chosen people were ***eleven days*** away from entering into the Promised Land when they left Egypt, ***eleven days*** away from the promise God had given, ***eleven days*** away from complete freedom from slavery. ***Eleven days*** . . . but ***forty years*** later . . .

Yes, the children of Israel wandered around the desert for forty years with a vision and a promise. Their faith was small. In spite of God's continued intervention, they doubted Him, believing only what they could see with their natural eyes. They were not sure where they were going or what they would find when they got there. They had only enough faith to follow Moses out of Egypt.

It took *forty years* before God finished weeding out those who would *never* allow ***"faith as a grain of mustard seed"*** or faith that *"acts like"* a grain of mustard seed to be developed in them. It took *forty years* before enough babies were born into freedom to realize that freedom was tangible. It took *forty years* to remove the ones who would rather travel around a mountain of *unbelief* than speak to it. These people *were moving* in their condition of *unbelief,* but *were not advancing* in the direction of their destiny.

You and I do not have another *forty years*. We must take this *eleven-day journey* for what it is. We must enter into the Promised Land in *eleven days* because we have an assignment. *Forty years* we

114   *Faith as . . .*

do not have. Eleven days we can handle. If we first allow *"faith as a grain of mustard seed"*, to be developed through our wilderness experience and deal with our mountain of *unbelief, eleven days* is all it will take and our journey will be complete.

You can spend as much time as you desire in the desert. You can build your idols, circle your mountain, or gripe and complain about any old thing you want. You can sit around and tell stories about how good it was back in Egypt; or you can get up, put on your walking shoes, *SPEAK TO* the mountain of *unbelief*, and possess your Promised Land.

Where are you now? Are you in Egypt or are you leaving Egypt? Have you been wandering around for ten or twenty years? Well, you can *stop now*. You know what the problem is. You know what obstacle stands between you and your destination. It is a mountain of *UNBELIEF*! *Unbelief* alone will stop you from entering into *your* Promised Land.

TODAY, IF YOU HEAR HIS VOICE

Hebrews 3:7-15

"Wherefore (as the Holy Ghost saith, To day if ye will hear his voice, harden not your hearts, as in the provocation, in the day of temptation in the wilderness: When your fathers tempted me, proved me, and saw my works forty years. Wherefore I was grieved with that generation, and said, They do alway err in their heart; and they have not known my

ways. So I sware in my wrath, They shall not enter into my rest.) Take heed, brethren, lest there be in any of you an evil heart of unbelief, in departing from the living God. But exhort one another daily, while it is called To day; lest any of you be hardened through the deceitfulness of sin. For we are made partakers of Christ, if we hold the beginning of our confidence stedfast unto the end; While it is said, To day if ye will hear his voice, harden not your hearts, as in the provocation."

Open your heart and mind to hear God. The children of Israel were God's chosen people, and some of them *could not* enter the Promised Land due to the *unbelief* in their hearts. The Israelites knew God was real and powerful. They had first-hand experience of miracles in the wilderness, but they did not recognize His voice when He spoke. Their hearts were hardened. They were uncomfortable with the way God was bringing things about, and it became their downfall. Do not allow this to happen to you.

"TODAY, if you will hear His voice. . ." *TODAY!* The Bible does not say *back then* you should have heard His voice. The Bible says *TODAY*; if you hear His voice, do not harden your hearts. Do not harden your hearts as in the rebellion and provocation. Do not become embittered in the day of testing. The children of Israel are an example of how *not* to listen to God. *You* must do the opposite. Listen to God; walk without rebellion through the tests that come your way; and allow the testing to develop *"faith as a grain of mustard seed"* or faith that *"acts like"* a grain of mustard seed, in you.

The children of Israel rebelled. What is rebellion? It is *"opposition to one in authority, an open, armed, and usually unsuccessful defiance or resistance to"*. In spite of rebellion, God was faithful and loving. God showed Himself faithful in protection, provision, and testing of His children. He wanted to prepare them for freedom. The children of Israel would no longer have man to dictate their every move. They needed to learn to *trust* God completely.

The children of Israel did not develop *"faith as a grain of mustard seed"* or faith that *"acts like"* a grain of mustard seed necessary to carry them through to the Promised Land. They kept looking back to *"the good ol' days"*. God allowed the ones most affected by a lifetime of bondage to die before bringing the rest of His people to freedom. The generation born in the wilderness only knew the wilderness. They did not know the false comfort of Egypt, so they were not drawn back to the *"good ol' days"* as were their ancestors.

The younger generation did have their share of problems, though. Their trouble was fear of being unable to conquer the giants in the Promised Land. They were able to see the abundance of all God had promised, but were afraid to move in and possess it.

You will most likely find yourself in one of these generations. Either you are always looking back to the past, or you are fearful of the giants in your future. What will be the result of your rebellion? What will be the result of your going astray? What will be the result of your failure to listen to God and develop *"faith as a grain of mustard seed"*? The results will be the same as they were for the children of

Israel. If you harden your heart and allow a mountain of *unbelief* to remain in your life, you will not enter into the Promised Land.

Hebrews 3:11

"Accordingly, I swore in My wrath and indignation, They shall not enter into My rest."

Unbelief produces no rest or peace. There is no way to *ENTER* into the things God has promised if you walk in *unbelief*. There is only wandering around in inner turmoil and anxiety in the wilderness until you and your promise die.

This is exactly the case with many people today. They go from dream to dream with lots of big ideas, never seeing them materialize. Inadvertently traveling in a circle and repeating the same crisis, they thrive on the drama a lifestyle of *unbelief* provides. Unable to receive correction and consistently blaming others for their problems, they are aggressive and confrontational. Intimidation is a key factor and the need to *always* be right keeps them poised to attack. Having no inner peace and no rest, they wander around in their unrest until they eventually self-destruct. God forbid!

Hebrews 3:12-13

"[Therefore beware] brethren, take care, lest there be in any one of you a wicked, unbelieving heart [which refuses to cleave to, trust in, and rely on Him], leading you to turn away and desert or stand aloof from the living God. But instead warn (admonish, urge, and encourage) one another every day, as long as it is called Today, that none of you may be

hardened [into settled rebellion] by the deceitfulness of sin [by the fraudulence, the stratagem, the trickery which the delusive glamor of his sin may play on him]". (Amplified Bible)

Take heed and do not allow yourself to develop a wicked and unbelieving heart that refuses to trust and rely on God. Warn one another every day, as long as it is called *Today*, so none will be hardened *(or settled into rebellion)* because of sin.

Hebrews 3:14

"For we have become fellows with Christ (the Messiah) and share in all He has for us, if only we hold our first newborn confidence and original assured expectation [in virtue of which we are believers] firm and unshaken to the end." (Amplified Bible)

BACK TO BONDAGE

The children of Israel, God's chosen people, complained, and wandered in the desert for forty long years. God delivered them from slavery, and they complained about that. They complained about the possibility of starving and then complained about the food God provided. They complained about being thirsty and then complained about the water God provided. They refused to submit to leadership, did not believe the prophetic word God gave them, and were disgruntled about most everything. They talked of how much better it was in Egypt. Imagine, babbling for bondage! They were complaining about their freedom from slavery.

Many people are complaining today. Spiritually, some people have spent much of their lives in slavery and bondage. When they are finally set free, they complain about circumstances and sometimes actually return to the things that had them bound.

Some of you complained while in bondage, complained when led out of bondage, and complained in the wilderness. Now that your promise is in view, you continue to complain. You say you should not have been in bondage; you were not brought out the way you expected; you did not see your promise fulfilled as quickly as you had hoped. When you finally do see your Promised Land, you complain that it might be too difficult to occupy. When this much time is spent complaining, you can rest assured no progress is being made to bring you into your destiny.

You may have some pre-conceived ideas about God and the way He should do things. If you are to do great things for *God*, it should be easy. Right? God, the creator of the universe, has chosen *YOU* to do a work! *Roll out the red carpet! Bring on the caviar! Calgon, take me away!* God has chosen to deliver you and bring you out of bondage into a land flowing with milk and honey. You expect that journey will be first class, short, and comfortable!

Is that *not* the way it is supposed to be? Should it *not* be quick and painless? No! Remember the race? It would be difficult to sit down and eat a steak dinner while running a race. While in transit, you may not have exactly what you want to eat, but God will provide manna. You would not dress in a three-piece suit to run a race, but God will not allow your running clothes to wear out. You may not have all of the money you think you should have for your race, but God will provide exactly what you need *EXACTLY* when you need it as He did for the children of Israel. They did not have the food they wanted, but they had the food they *needed*. Their clothes did not wear out. They lacked nothing *and* they were free! Still, they complained, and it cost them. It cost some of them their promise altogether. They *never* entered the Promised Land. Those who finally did enter were delayed due to *unbelief*.

COMPLAINING CAUSES CRISIS'

Numbers 12:1-2

"And Miriam and Aaron spake against Moses because of the Ethiopian woman whom he had married: for he had married an Ethiopian woman. And they said, Hath the LORD indeed spoken only by Moses? hath he not spoken also by us? And the LORD heard it."

Miriam, the sister of Moses, was a prophetess and a leader of praise and worship, but she was stricken with leprosy and cast outside the camp for seven days. The journey of three to six million people was *delayed* for seven days because of *ONE* person's *unbelief*. Miriam and Aaron, sister and brother of Moses, had spoken against Moses because of his Ethiopian wife, but Moses' wife was not the issue. In **Numbers 12: 2** the Bible says, *"and they* (Miriam and Aaron) *said, 'Has the Lord indeed spoken only by Moses? Hath He not spoken also by us?' And the Lord heard it."* GOD heard their complaining and saw what was in their hearts. Not only were they questioning the man God had placed in authority over them, they were jealous. God had things under control, and Moses was in charge. All the decisions Moses made, including his choice of a wife, were between him and God.

God chose Miriam and Aaron to help Moses, but they had a problem with rebellion, especially Miriam. The people followed Miriam in praise and worship and into the presence of God. Without God's intervention in the matter, how long would it be before they followed her into rebellion and *unbelief?* Miriam had *unbelief* in her heart. Maybe she did not believe God had placed her in that position to fulfill her destiny.

Numbers 12:6-8

"And he said, Hear now my words: If there be a prophet among you, I the LORD will make myself known unto him in a vision, and will speak unto him in a dream. My servant Moses is not so, who is faithful in all mine house. With him will I speak mouth to mouth, even apparently, and not in dark speeches; and the similitude of the LORD shall he behold: wherefore then were ye not afraid to speak against my servant Moses?"

God called Moses, Miriam, and Aaron out. He came down and stood in the door of the tabernacle, in the pillar of the cloud and called Aaron and Miriam forth. God had something to say. He told them; this is not simply another prophet that I speak to in dreams and visions, this is *Moses*. He is faithful. I speak openly and directly to him, and he sees My form. Why were you *not afraid* to speak against him?

It could have been partly because Moses was their brother. Maybe it was their familiarity with him. Moses was a man and he had shortcomings as everyone does, but God handpicked him. The Bible says Moses was *meek* above all men. God knew what He had deposited in Moses, but Miriam and Aaron had allowed their unbelieving hearts to cause them to speak against God's chosen servant. Those who were closest to leadership were *the ones who began to speak against the leadership.*

Numbers 12:10-16

"And the cloud departed from off the tabernacle; and, behold, Miriam became leprous, white as snow: and Aaron looked upon Miriam, and, behold, she was leprous. And Aaron said unto Moses, Alas, my lord, I beseech thee, lay not the sin upon us, wherein we have done foolishly, and wherein we have sinned. Let her not be as one dead, of whom the flesh is half consumed when he cometh out of his mother's womb. And Moses cried unto the LORD, saying, Heal her now, O God, I beseech thee. And the LORD said unto Moses, If her father had but spit in her face, should she not be ashamed seven days? let her be shut out from the camp seven days, and after that let her be received in again. And Miriam was shut out from the camp seven days: and the people journeyed not till Miriam was brought in again. And afterward the people removed from Hazeroth, and pitched in the wilderness of Paran."

God knew the hearts of both Miriam and Aaron. Miriam was stricken with leprosy. When Aaron looked at her, she was leprous. Why not Miriam and Aaron? Both had spoken against Moses.

It was Aaron though, who was repentant for his actions. Aaron immediately recognizes how foolishly they acted and confesses to Moses. He not only repented for himself, but Miriam also. Moses also spoke on Miriam's behalf. Moses intercedes for Miriam's immediate healing, yet she is sent out of the camp for seven days.

Notice, Miriam never acknowledged her sin. She said absolutely nothing. She was stricken with leprosy, sent out of the camp seven days, received in again, and the journey continued. This one woman's rebellious, complaining, and unbelieving attitude held up the journey of the whole congregation for seven days.

Leprosy begins with a sore underneath the skin and spreads; ultimately, pieces of the body literally *FALL* off! When you allow *unbelief* to cause you to rebel and speak against leadership, you may not see anything happen immediately. Rebellion is contagious and it soon spreads. When rebellion spreads, pieces of the body (*or ministry*) begin to *"fall off"*. People have trouble working together; unity goes out the window; strife comes through the door; jealousy erupts; and progress to a *God-given destiny* is all but stopped. All of this transpires because *unbelief* is permitted and rebellion settles in. Rebellion is sin and sin separates you from God. Think about it!

Isaiah 59:2

"But your iniquities have separated between you and your God, and your sins have hid his face from you, that he will not hear."

Guard yourself. Do not complain, express dissatisfaction or protest against leadership. This is a manifestation of *unbelief.* If you are complaining about your situation, the way God is handling your affairs, or His timing, you are walking in *unbelief.* If you are protesting against the person or persons God is using in leadership, you are walking in rebellion and *unbelief.* Please understand. *UNBELIEF* is the root problem. *UNBELIEF* will cause you and others around you to experience a delay in reaching your destiny.

Unbelief can only be dealt with by allowing ***"faith as a grain of mustard seed"*** or faith that *"acts like"* a grain of mustard seed to be developed in you. ***"Faith as a grain of mustard seed"*** or faith that *"acts like"* a grain of mustard seed develops through a process. The *"Mustard Seed Process"*. You must to understand *"The Mustard Seed Process"* before you can accept where you are and what you are going through as a part of God's ultimate plan. Once you understand there is a *process,* you will accept your role in God's plan and receive His leadership. Only then will you fully understand that all He has provided is *ALL* you need.

10

THE MUSTARD SEED PROCESS

THE CRUSHING

In order to go where others have not gone, you must do what others have not been willing to do. You must also decide whether you are willing to go through *the process* required to get you there. Will you yield yourself to God and allow Him to complete the "Mustard Seed Process" in you?

First, you need to learn about the mustard seed. If you learn how a mustard seed *"acts"*, you will better understand the "Mustard Seed Process". A mustard seed is no ordinary seed.

I will share with you what I have learned about this mustard seed and its characteristics. Through this, you will discover what it means to have **"faith as a grain of mustard seed"** or faith that *"acts like"* a grain of mustard seed.

In Jesus' time on earth, farmers crushed the tiny mustard seeds before they sowed them in the earth. Someone discovered, if crushed, the already tiny seed would produce double. Yes, if these small seeds were crushed, they would produce double!

The seed on the inside of you may look like any other seed, but it is an uncommon seed. The seed in you is the *Word of God* both written and spoken. God wants your seed to produce *as* the mustard seed. He not only wants you to produce; He wants you to produce double! He wants to give you double for your trouble! For your shame, the Lord says He will give you double! For all the trouble you have been through, the Lord says He will give you double. Will you accept double for the trouble you have experienced? I will gladly take double for my trouble, and be happy!

Wait a minute, though. Do not miss this. Did you see the word *crush?* You must be **crushed** to produce double! You are not sure about *that*, are you? You have been through enough and now you have to be **crushed** before you can produce your full potential? You may feel as though more *crushing* would destroy you. You may question, is *crushing* necessary? Jesus said you must have **"faith as a grain of mustard seed"** or faith that *"acts like"* a grain of mustard seed. The first thing the farmers did to the little mustard seed was, *crush* it. Yes, it looks as though you must be crushed. If not, you may produce, but it will *not* be what you are capable of producing. *DOUBLE!*

As someone who has experienced *"crushing"*, you are probably wincing as you read these words. Crushing is unpleasant and

128 *Faith as ...*

painful, but the pain does not last forever. It is only *part* of the "Mustard Seed Process", not the whole process. Be encouraged! Not one person in the Bible that produced for the Lord escaped crushing. Joseph's life is a good example of crushing.

JOSEPH'S CRUSHING EXPERIENCE

Joseph's life virtually began with crushing. His mother died when he was young, and his father was old. His brothers misbehaved every time they got out of their father's sight, but Joseph was attentive and obedient. Joseph was loved and favored by his father. His father so favored Joseph that he gave him a special coat designed with many colors, but the special treatment he received caused his brothers to hate him.

Have you been hated by people because your Father God showed His favor and loving kindness to you by blessing your life? This can be a crushing experience. You want to be accepted and loved. Sometimes, however, people get jealous of God's favor on you and desire you to be miserable. Some will try to kill your vision! They will allow themselves to be used by the devil to attempt to keep you from reaching your destiny. As in Joseph's case, it is often members of your immediate family or those most trusted, causing you the most opposition.

God gave Joseph dreams. Through these dreams, he realized he would be in an exalted position in the future. Notice, however, God did **not** show Joseph the *crushing* that would come first. God gave

Joseph a dream *or vision* to hold on to as a *"joy set before him"* to offset the trouble to come, because trouble was definitely coming!

Joseph's brothers hated him to begin with, but after they learned of his dreams, they wanted to kill him. Instead, they sold him into slavery for approximately twelve dollars and eighty cents! His father was heart-broken. He thought Joseph was dead. Joseph's situation did not look good and definitely did not look anything like the dreams God had given him. God was in control though, and He allowed things to happen in Joseph's life to place him on the proper path to his destiny.

Joseph was sold in Egypt to Potiphar, an officer of Pharoah and captain of the guard. God's favor was on Joseph, and Potiphar set him over his entire house. Potiphar trusted and favored Joseph, but Potiphar's wife made advances toward him. Joseph, being a man of integrity, who honored God, knew how much Potiphar trusted him and he refused her advances. She accused Joseph of making advances toward her, and he was thrust into prison. This was yet *another* crushing experience. Joseph had done nothing to deserve this. Nevertheless, God was in control, because Joseph *could* have been executed for that accusation!

While in prison, God's favor positioned Joseph in a place of authority. When the Pharoah's butler and baker were imprisoned with Joseph, he had an opportunity to interpret their dreams. The interpretation was that the baker would be hanged and the butler restored to Pharoah. All Joseph asked was to be *remembered* and brought out of prison when the butler was restored to Pharoah. After his restoration, the butler *FORGOT* Joseph, and he remained in prison. *More crushing!* The butler remembered Joseph though, *two years* later! Pharoah needed an interpretation for *his* dream. Joseph interpreted Pharoah's dream regarding the seven years of plenty and the seven years of famine to come. When he did so, Pharoah placed Joseph over his house and all the land of Egypt. Pharoah placed a ring, a chain and fine clothes on Joseph. He was now second only to Pharoah. Joseph had certainly been crushed, but he was now prepared to produce *"double"* and go on to reach his destiny.

During the time of famine, Joseph's brothers came to Egypt for food. They bowed before Joseph, yet they did not recognize him. God had brought to pass the dream He had given Joseph many years ago. Joseph remembered the dream, but his brothers did not. Joseph remembered because, holding on to the vision God had given him was the thing that carried him through the *"crushing"* he experienced. You cannot expect others to remember or hold on to *your* vision. You are the only one who can truly appreciate the vision God has given you. After long periods of time, you are likely the only one the dream or vision remains alive in.

Joseph was a man who had favor with God, but was crushed. Not once or twice, but every time Joseph turned around, he was being mistreated, falsely accused or forgotten. Joseph would have qualified as an *expert* on crushing!

There are many who have been crushed, but *"crushing"* is only part of a more extensive process used to equip you to produce for

God. *Remember*, the Lord is preparing you to produce *double*. He is preparing you to receive *double for your trouble*! All of the hard things happening in your personal life, family, and ministry will cause you to grow to maturity and produce twice as much. Just as the little mustard seed was crushed, *you* will be. After the crushing though, the little mustard seed grew into twice the plant with twice the root system, producing twice the fruit! You will also.

Do not give up! Crushing is only the beginning; you must continue through the entire "Mustard Seed Process". Allow God to use the crushing to develop *"faith as a grain of mustard seed"* or faith that *"acts like"* a grain of mustard seed in you and prepare you to produce double.

ORDINARY IS OUT

How often have you looked at someone's walk with the Lord and said, *"That is what I want to be!"* They have gone through the process it takes to develop *"faith as a grain of mustard seed"* or faith that *"acts like"* a grain of mustard seed. Their faith has grown into true *"faith as a grain of mustard seed"*. They are producing double for the Lord and you can too, but you cannot get there doing the same old things you have always done. Leave *ordinary* things behind. It may mean stepping out of your comfort zone, leaving others behind or doing what is right instead of what *"feels good"*. Refusal to accept change, cleaving to ungodly relationships rooted in rebellion or control and gratifying the *"flesh"* are all signs of ordinary seeds. These decisions pull you down and cause you to forfeit or walk away from your destiny.

Some people allow a *"religious spirit"* to operate through them and keep them from developing. This spirit attempts to turn you away from your vision and stop you short of developing to full potential. A religious spirit does not want you to be successful in your endeavors for the *Kingdom of God.* Your *success* may cause those operating under the influence of this spirit to feel inadequate or inferior. They have the same potential you have to grow and produce but lack the drive necessary to continue through the process to develop ***"faith as a grain of mustard seed"*** or faith that *"acts like"* a grain of mustard seed. Instead of acquiring that level of faith, they will attempt to *hinder* you. They whittle away at you in order to control how far you grow. A religious spirit appears to be doing all the *right* things, but is unwilling to *"pay the price"*. People entertaining this spirit refuse to go through the process required to bring them to the level of excellence God intends. As you move forward, they sit in judgment of you, assaulting you with accusations that you are going nowhere. A person with a religious spirit will attempt to convince you that you are not growing spiritually, when actually, it is *their* growth that is stunted. If allowed to influence you, their manipulation may become the obstacle that trips you, knocking the wind out of you, taking your zeal and fire, stopping you short of your destiny.

In order to have ***"faith as a grain of mustard seed"*** or faith that *"acts like"* a grain of mustard seed and complete the "Mustard Seed Process", you must not allow a religious spirit to operate in you.

Allowing religion in any form is out. Submission to the Holy Spirit is in. You cannot be ordinary in your conviction, faith, or drive to reach your destiny. Be tenacious in your quest for the accomplishment of God's plan in your life. Make up your mind to allow *"faith as a grain of mustard seed"* or faith that *"acts like"* a grain of mustard seed to be developed in you.

The Word the Lord has spoken over your life is for *you*. It is *your* vision. You are the one who must complete the "Mustard Seed Process". Do not miss your destiny because of another's lack of *"faith as a grain of mustard seed"* and remember, *ordinary is out!*

ALL SEEDS START IN DARKNESS

All seeds, whether natural or spiritual, start out in darkness. All seeds, whether ordinary or extraordinary begin at the same place. The natural seed is dropped into the ground, covered with dirt, and watered. For a while, the seed lies dormant. It looks as though nothing is happening. The seed must die and then the growth process begins. Seeds instinctively reach for the light. If conditions are conducive to growth, the seed will grow. Often, seeds will encounter obstacles during the growth process. If a seed is an ordinary seed, it will quit growing when it meets an obstruction.

Your spiritual seed starts in darkness, also. When you surrender your heart to the Lord, the seed within begins the growth process. Your seed instinctively reaches for your Father God. When first saved, some people think they are perfected immediately, but they have only begun a process with many stages and many obstacles to overcome.

Die to yourself and conform to the image of Christ. Be careful not to become like the ordinary, natural seed that meets with an obstacle and cannot continue. If this happens, *"faith as a grain of mustard seed"* or faith that *"acts like"* a grain of mustard seed will not develop. Do not allow this. Remember, your seed is no *ordinary* seed.

If you plant a seed in the ground you cannot *see* it growing, but that does not mean it is not developing properly. Much of the vital growth takes place underneath the soil, in the darkness, and out of sight.

Do you want to have *"faith as a grain of mustard seed"* or faith that *"acts like"* a grain of mustard seed fully developed in you? Will you go through whatever process is necessary to reach the level of *faith* needed to finish the race and reach your destiny? In order to do this, you must see things from God's perspective. God's plan rarely looks like *you* think it should.

THE KINGDOM OF GOD IS LIKE A MUSTARD SEED

Mark 4:30-31

"Jesus said whereunto shall we liken the kingdom of God or with what comparison shall we compare it. He said it is like a grain of mustard seed which when it is sown in the earth is less than all the seeds that be in the earth, but when it is sown it groweth up and becometh greater than all herbs and shooteth out

great branches so that the fowls of the air may lodge under the shadow of it."

Jesus said the *Kingdom of God* is like a grain of mustard seed. He asks, **"whereunto** (*or to what place or purpose*) **shall we liken the Kingdom of God or with what comparison shall we compare it"**? Then He teaches us. **"It is like a grain of mustard seed, which, when it is sown in the earth, is less than all the seeds that be in the earth"**. What *earth* is He referring to in this passage? The earth is *YOU!*

The seed *(the Word of God)* planted in you, begins as **"less than all other seeds"**. It may be pushed down by the cares of the world. It may go unnoticed, be forgotten, go unattended, or have weeds growing all around it. Your seed is a tiny little thing. It needs to be cultivated, nurtured, and allowed to mature. Then, when it is sown deep in *your earth*, though it is the least of all seeds, it has the possibility of becoming larger and producing more than any other seed. When **"faith as a grain of mustard seed"** or faith that *"acts like"* a grain of mustard seed is fully developed, it will grow into a tree. Your faith will develop a strong root system, will produce double, be double in strength and a shelter for others.

Many are looking for a place to take refuge. Is your **"faith as a grain of mustard seed"** or faith that *"acts like"* a grain of mustard seed developed enough to help someone else? Are your *faith* branches thick and healthy enough to provide shelter? Could you help to support another Christian in a time of need? Does your *faith* root system go deep enough to keep *you* from being uprooted? It is imperative you allow *"faith as a grain of mustard seed"* or faith that *"acts like"* a grain of mustard seed to be developed in you.

THE DYING

As you go through the "Mustard Seed Process", you may say, "I know I have been crushed"! Finally, there is an explanation for all the agony! You now know the *crushing* is part of the *process* and it is working to develop *"faith as a grain of mustard seed"* or faith that *"acts like"* a grain of mustard seed in you, but where do you go from here? What is the next step?

Seeds are planted and then die before they sprout and become full-grown plants. The outer part of a seed must break and fall apart before the actual growth takes place.

In the natural, the mustard seed is planted in the dark, damp soil and left to die. When the soil is prepared for planting, it is loose. After a while, the sun beats down, the rain comes, and the soil packs down solid. It may seem an eternity before the plant shoots forth into the light!

You have seen your destiny, but you too must experience a dying out to *"self"*. You have seen a vision of the direction and the call of God on your life, but then, when you thought it was about to come to pass, you see it die. This is not a quick and painless death; but a slow, decaying, dying-out, falling apart process so painful you do not know if you will recover.

The vision God has placed in you is buried beneath a pile of dirt. It is beginning to decay and it smells! What heartache and what loss you feel. Everything you had hoped for, every plan you had made, every dream you had believed in is lying beneath the cold, hard ground rotting away. You want to quit. You feel as though more is being piled on than you can bear. It is through *this* death process that God will fulfill *HIS* vision in you. Die to yourself and your ideas, and God will revive you and show you HIS plan.

This is a good time to shout and rejoice! Do not wait until the battle is over! Shout now! Dance in advance! *Yes!* Your seed is under the soil. *Yes!* You have been completely crushed, and *now* you are dying, but rejoice! You are another step closer to having *"faith as a grain of mustard seed"* or faith that *"acts like"* a grain of mustard seed developed in you!

THE WATERING

Now comes the watering. The watering part of the "Mustard Seed Process" should encourage you. The watering is a spiritual river sent by the Holy Spirit to revive you. God sometimes sends others to water you spiritually. He may send someone with a Word of encouragement or with reproof. Words of encouragement are easier to accept, but when someone comes to water your seed with reproof, it is more difficult. Instead of encouraging you, it can add more weight to your already pressed condition.

You do not know how you will produce at all, much less produce double. It seems too difficult, but you *must* accept reproof. **Proverbs 10:17** tells us, *"He is in the way of life that keepeth instruction: but he that refuseth reproof erreth."* When you yield yourself completely to God, there will be crushing, burying, dying, and heavy, heavy soil; but underneath the dirt, life springs forth, and hope begins to grow.

Okay, you say, maybe there is a reason for this difficult process. Maybe all of this crushing, dying, and watering *will* turn into something good. Your little, crushed mustard seed, your *"faith as a grain of mustard seed"* or faith that *"acts like"* a grain of mustard seed has begun to develop. Though it cannot be seen, there is life and an instinct inside of the seed to continue reaching for light.

After being crushed, buried, and nearly drowned, ordinary seeds will stop growing. When ordinary seeds come up against an obstacle, they push against it reaching for light; but when they cannot move through or press past the obstacle, they die. The ordinary seed gives up, but not the mustard seed.

When the little mustard seed comes up against an obstacle, it presses and presses. If it cannot get to the light, instead of dying like ordinary everyday, run-of-the-mill, common seeds, it begins to grow. Against all odds, it begins growing under and around the obstacle. The mustard seed keeps growing and growing and growing. It grows up and down. It winds in and out, around and around. There is no obstacle able to stop the mustard seed from reaching for the light. It continues to grow until it finds a way around whatever obstacle is in its path. Though it may seem to be the long way around, this process of changing directions and continuing to press, is developing an extensive root system.

THE ROOT SYSTEM

While the mustard plant is forming its root system, it looks as if nothing is happening on the surface. This little seed is making its way around obstacle after obstacle in the dark, and no one can *see* any movement. It does not *look* like *anything* is happening.

It looks this way when your ***"faith as a grain of mustard seed"*** or faith that *"acts like"* a grain of mustard seed is being developed. As you press on, overcoming obstacle after obstacle, no one can *see* what is developing in you. Sometimes *you* are not able to see changes yourself. All you know is darkness, dampness, and constant pressing. You keep reaching, hoping you will break through the heavy layer of soil lying over you. Others around you may be looking at the surface of your life, unable also to see the changes taking place deep within. Although, not seen, the seed keeps growing this way and that developing a strong root system until a plant shoots forth. By this time, the root system is strong enough to cause it to grow up greater than all other plants.

Many want to be greater than all others, but they do not want to go through the process required. Some will come this far but will be unable to make it through dry times. Nothing short of developing ***"faith as a grain of mustard seed"*** or faith that *"acts like"* a grain of mustard seed will be powerful enough to carry you through a season of drought. You *must* know in whom to place your trust and hope.

TIMES OF DROUGHT

Jeremiah 17:7-8

"Blessed is the man that trusteth in the LORD, and whose hope the LORD is. For he shall be as a tree planted by the waters, and that spreadeth out her roots by the river, and shall not see when heat cometh, but her leaf shall be green; and shall not be careful in the year of drought, neither shall cease from yielding fruit!"

Inevitably, times of drought will come. There will be times when the waters of encouragement and reproof would be a welcome sight. During these *"dry"* times, you may feel as though your prayers are not reaching God.

Do not be discouraged. If your root system is well developed, you will not dry up. In times of drought, your leaves will not wither. When everybody around you is dry and cracked, you will stand strong and flourish. You are drawing water from a deeper source. You are blessed because your trust and hope is in the Lord.

REJECT A ROOT OF REJECTION

Do not place your trust in man. Man can and will reject you but God has accepted you. The reason you receive or entertain a spirit of rejection is, *UNBELIEF*. You do not fully believe you are accepted into the beloved. Avoid developing a root of rejection.

Realize though, *some* rejection is healthy. Did you know your role model Jesus was rejected by all men? Do you want to be great in the *Kingdom of God*? If so, you can count on a great deal of rejection in this lifetime. Do not allow rejection to stop you from reaching your destiny. You must not allow rejection to cause your root system to rot.

The father of the demon-possessed young man spoken of in chapter seven, could have easily allowed a spirit of rejection to attach itself to him. Jesus' disciples prayed for his son to be delivered, but nothing happened. Yes, this father could have felt rejected. He could have said, "Why me? Why not me? Why, why, why?" However, he did not allow a root of rejection to cultivate. When the father did not see results, he pressed on. He did not give up. He continued until he drew the attention of the One he *KNEW* was able to resolve his problem, Jesus Christ Himself. The man did not know why the disciples could not cure his son, but he was determined to press on and find the One who *could*!

BREAKING THROUGH

Do you have the perseverance to complete the process that develops ***"faith as a grain of mustard seed"*** or faith that *"acts like"* a grain of mustard seed?

When the call of God is realized in your life, you may say, *"God, I will do whatever you have called me to do. I will go wherever you have called me to go. I will say whatever you instruct me to say."* Maybe you think you can do it with "Teeny-Weeny Faith", "Plain, Old, Ordinary Faith", or "Overcoming Faith". Realize it is impossible without the crushing, dying, watering, changing direction, pressing in, drawing from a deeper source, avoiding a root of rejection *faith* to do what God has called you to do! It takes *"faith as a grain of mustard seed"*. If you have faith that *"acts like"*, has the same characteristics of, and is *"determined"* like this little mustard seed, *then* you will produce what the mustard seed produces. *DOUBLE!* Then *"nothing shall be impossible unto you"*.

11

NOTHING IS IMPOSSIBLE

DEAL WITH THE MOUNTAIN!

If you have *"faith as a grain of mustard seed"* or faith that *"acts like"* a grain of mustard seed, you can *say* to the mountain of *unbelief*, *"Remove! Get out of my life! Get out of my mind! Get out of my thinking! Loose me in Jesus' name!"* If you have gone through the *"Mustard Seed Process"* and allowed *"faith as a grain of mustard seed"* or faith that *"acts like"* a grain of mustard seed to be developed in you, you can SAY to the mountain of *unbelief*, *"Remove to yonder place"* and *it will move!* Jesus said the mountain would obey you. Once the mountain of *unbelief* moves, your problems will move also. Any illness, poverty, fear, hatred, or despair must bow to the name of Jesus, but first, you *must* deal with *unbelief*. God has called you to produce in the earth, and you must go forth and produce.

Unbelief is a strong spirit designed to keep you where you are. Implemented by the devil, it will keep your feet nailed to the floor so you *NEVER* accomplish all that God has given you to do. It is designed to keep your family lost and headed for hell, to bring wedges in relationships, and set up jealousy and competition between people. The devil does not care if you go to church, as long as he can render you ineffective with *unbelief.*

Many of you have struggled year after year and your situation has gotten worse. You have felt hopeless. You have had faith for other people, but not for *YOURSELF*. This description of you may have been correct in the past, but do not allow it to determine your future! God has *unveiled unbelief* and shown you the process by which *"faith as a grain of mustard seed"* or faith that *"acts like"* a grain of mustard seed is developed. When you finish this process, you will finish the race and reach your destiny, and *NOTHING* shall be impossible for you!

PREPARE TO PRAY *AND* FAST

You have learned of the process by which *"faith as a grain of mustard seed"* or faith that *"acts like"* a grain of mustard seed is developed, but you may be asking yourself what steps can be taken to ensure steadfastness *during* the process.

Prayer and fasting are key elements that go hand in hand, with all you have learned thus far. Applying the principles of prayer and fasting will assist in power to cast out demons, heal offenses, root out rejection, and move a mountain of *unbelief!* You will be awakened spiritually and begin to see things from God's perspective. Prayer and fasting are two of the most powerful Christian disciplines. Through them, the Holy Spirit will transform your life!

Prayer and fasting are important when dealing with *unbelief*. Jesus said in **Mark 9:28-29,** ***"This kind, goeth not out except by prayer and fasting".*** What did Jesus mean when He said, *"this kind"?* He meant *unbelief*! The spirit of *UNBELIEF*!

Remember, *unbelief* is a strong spirit, affecting many people, preventing them from reaching the destiny God has for them. Examine yourself for a moment. What kind of relationship do you have with the Lord? Does *unbelief* play a role in your walk with the Lord? When was the last time you set yourself to fast? How is your prayer life?

Is your time with the Lord sporadic and uneventful or disciplined and full of exciting activity each day? Realize you have an enemy whose goal is to deter you and cause you to lose focus. Prayer and fasting is the key to developing ***"faith as a grain of mustard seed"*** or faith that *"acts like"* a grain of mustard seed and casting out *unbelief*.

If you do not already know the power and importance of prayer and fasting, here are some basics. Prayer and fasting will result in a more intimate relationship with Christ and enables the Holy Spirit to reveal your true spiritual condition. Seeing yourself from God's perspective will result in brokenness, repentance and transformation. The Holy Spirit will quicken the *Word of God* in your heart and His truth will become more meaningful. Fasting will transform your prayer life into a richer more intimate experience and will result in a personal revival overflowing into the lives of others. When you fast,, your spirit man rules and refuses under the control of the Holy Spirit to give place to the flesh.

Prayer and fasting is a biblical way to humble oneself. As David said in Psalm 35:13, *"I humbled my soul with fasting"*. Though his enemies were falsely accusing him, David prayed for them when they were sick, he fasted and mourned for them, as he would have for his brother or mother. Though they mistreated him, David's heart was right before God concerning his enemies.

Many suffer mistreatment, but picking up the telephone to relate your pain to a friend or using the pulpit to make sure everyone knows how bad it is, is not the way to handle the situation. Go before God in prayer and fasting with the right motives and a repentant heart. Humble yourself before God and He will hear and answer your prayer. Pray for your accusers rather than meditating on how badly you have been hurt. In so doing, you will release yourself from the past and equip yourself with power to embrace the future.

II Chronicles 7:14

"If my people, who are called by my name, will humble themselves and pray and seek my face and turn from their wicked ways, then will I hear from heaven and will forgive their sin and will heal their land."

God said in **II Chronicles 7:14**, if *HIS* people, who are called by *HIS* name, will humble themselves and pray and seek *HIS* face and turn from their wicked ways, He will hear them, forgive and heal their land. *What a Word!* Realize also, when God spoke this Word, he was not speaking to sinners, but to *His* people.

As you humble yourself before God and pray, confess *all* sin, as He reveals it. Recognize and place sins of *omission* as well as sins of *commission* under the blood of Jesus Christ by faith. Examine yourself closely for pride, worldly thinking, spiritual indifference, self-centeredness, insufficient time in God's Word, and lack of prayer. Confess your sins as the Holy Spirit brings them to your attention and continue to focus on God and God alone in order for your prayers to be powerful and effective. As He leads you into repentance of unconfessed sin, you will recognize the *unbelief* operating in your life. Through continued prayer and fasting, *unbelief* will be *unveiled* and rooted out.

Mark 9:28-29

"And when he was come into the house, his disciples asked him privately, Why could not we cast him out? And he said unto them, This kind can come forth by nothing, but by prayer and fasting."

As mentioned earlier, the Bible says in **Mark 9:28-29** that Jesus' disciples asked Him about their inability to cast out the demon from the young man. Maybe the disciples had been busy and neglected prayer time, but the Bible also says earlier in the book of **Mark** that they *had not fasted.* They had not been instructed to fast at that time, but Jesus *did* say the time would come when they *would* fast.

Mark 2:18-20

" And the disciples of John and of the Pharisees used to fast: and they come and say unto him, Why do the disciples of John and of the Pharisees fast, but thy disciples fast not? And Jesus said unto them, Can the children of the bridechamber fast, while the bridegroom is with them? as long as they have the bridegroom with them, they cannot fast. But the days will come, when the bridegroom shall be taken away from them, and then shall they fast in those days. "

Witnessing the miracles Jesus performed should have been enough to show His disciples the important role fasting would play in their lives. Jesus was their example. He was in constant communication with the Father and He fasted, but His disciples were slow in their understanding. Although not instructed to fast, Jesus' disciples *did* take note of His prayer life and asked Him to teach them to pray.

Luke 11:1

"And it came to pass, that, as he was praying in a certain place, when he ceased, one of his disciples said unto him, Lord, teach us to pray, as John also taught his disciples".

They were learning and making an effort to understand, but things were happening quickly. They knew about prayer, and had seen many miracles, but they were about to learn something new.

The disciples prayed for deliverance for the young man, but gave up too soon! They prayed for him, but prayed only *once*. The young man had been in this condition since he was a child. Could the father have related his story to the disciples? Did he give the disciples more information than they needed? Did it hinder their faith? Could they have heard the father explaining how long this trial had gone on and how severely this condition had affected his son?

Due to the fast paced, ever growing ministry, they may have lost their focus and begun to see situations from a natural standpoint. Maybe they gave too much credence to the young man's condition and stopped short in their prayer.

When flesh controls, you quit too soon regarding spiritual things and hold fast too long to fleshly matters. The nature of the flesh is to be lazy, self-serving, rebellious, selfish, and arrogant. You will never see results when you pray prayers based on carnal knowledge and fleshly desires. This happened to Jesus' disciples. They prayed for the young man once, and moved on. They tried, but to no avail. They could not produce the promise for this desperate family, although they had power over all devils and disease. Their lack of understanding and confusion was evident when they later sought answers from Jesus regarding this situation.

The characteristic of the flesh is to always look for the easy way out. The flesh is weak and will influence you to give up too soon when dealing with anything that takes effort such as praying and fasting. It will also hold on too long to unnecessary, unproductive, and inappropriate things such as murmuring and complaining. When influenced by the flesh, you want to understand or *fix* things in your natural strength. If allowed, the flesh will persuade you to desperately hold to past hurts and offenses. This type of indulgence, is a breeding ground for *unbelief* and will be detrimental to reaching your destiny. Understand, you must not allow your flesh to govern your life.

The disciples prayed once and walked away: They *should* have been persistent. According to **Luke Chapter 18**, *"men ought always to pray and not to faint"*. No matter what the circumstances or how long the situation had gone on they should have continued to pray until they saw results. Instead, *unbelief* caused them to miss an opportunity for victory. You *must not* give up after only one prayer. You may be giving up the moment before you receive your miracle!

Luke 18:1-8

" And he spake a parable unto them to this end, that men ought always to pray, and not to faint; Saying, There was in a city a judge, which feared not God, neither regarded man: And there was a widow in that city; and she came unto him, saying, Avenge me of mine adversary. And he would not for a while: but afterward he said within himself, Though I fear not God, nor regard man; Yet because this widow troubleth me, I will avenge her, lest by her continual coming she weary me. And the Lord said, Hear what the unjust judge saith. And shall not God avenge his own elect, which cry day and night unto him, though he bear long with them? I tell you that he will avenge them speedily. Nevertheless when the Son of man cometh, shall he find faith on the earth?"

As the woman who went to the unjust judge, you should *continue* to seek God and *continue* to pray and ask. If the unjust judge granted the woman what she asked, how much more will God do for His children? God is aware of every need, but sometimes He waits for you to become conscious of how desperately you need Him. Desperate people, who know their only help is God, will stay focused and seek the ways of the Spirit until they see results. Not all desperate people have decided to seek the ways of righteousness as their avenue of deliverance. Many continue in their desperation on the broad road to destruction. For those who have made up their minds, though, it is not easy to sway them from the straight and narrow path that leads to their desire.

James 5:16

" . . . The effectual fervent prayer of a righteous man availeth much. "

Seek the Lord with sincerity of heart. Live righteous, or *"in right standing"* with God, because **James 5:16** says, ***"The effectual, fervent prayer of a righteous man availeth much"***.

The book of **I Kings,** teaches how Elijah prayed it would not rain and it did not. It also teaches how he then prayed that it *would* rain and it did.

James 5:17

"Elias was a man subject to like passions as we are, and he prayed earnestly that it might not rain: and it rained not on the earth by the space of three years and six months".

The Bible says that he was a man like you and me, with **"like passions"**. He had the same intense emotions compelling him to action. He had the same zeal and enthusiasm as you and I. Yet, he was a man, and had to overcome his flesh the same as everyone.

During the time of Elijah, King Ahab reigned and married a Phoenician princess named Jezebel. Jezebel was a highly gifted and extremely powerful woman. She was also exceedingly evil. She kept company and worshiped with four hundred and fifty prophets of Baal *(a pagan god of storms and fertility whose name literally means "owner", "master", or "husband")*. Elijah experienced great victory over those prophets of Baal by calling down fire from heaven to consume a sacrifice drenched in water. He then had the prophets of Baal killed. Jezebel being the evil woman she was, then threatened the life of Elijah.

When you read the Bible further, you will discover how fear of man *(or mankind)*, which is a manifestation of the flesh, caused Elijah to run and hide. How could this happen? Jezebel was a woman and Elijah a *powerful* man of God. You will discover that Elijah fasted for forty days and after he fasted, he did not run from Jezebel or anyone else again, *ever*!

Elijah was a man of God who struggled the same as you and I, but remember he was a *praying* and *fasting* man. Elijah knew God heard his prayers. He knew God could and would do mighty works. He was faithful to fast and persistent in prayer and God heard and delivered him.

FASTING - WHAT IS IT?

What *is* fasting? The word *"fast"* in the dictionary means, *"to abstain from food"*. In the Greek language, to *"fast"* means *"to shut your mouth to food"*. In Hebrew, it means, *"to cover the mouth with the hand and abstain from food"*. What many call fasting is not fasting at all. They choose some sort of discipline such as abstaining from watching TV, reading the newspaper or sports and call it fasting. According to the true meaning of fasting, unless you eat televisions, snack on the daily newspaper, or have baseballs with your meal instead of rolls, you are not fasting. Although, *any* discipline in which you focus on the Lord is good, you can certainly be deceived if not careful. The enemy does not want you to fast according to the Bible because fasting produces great power. Fasting *unveils* and *deals* with *unbelief*. When you and I deal with *unbelief*, the power of God is revealed in our lives. Fasting not only opens up pathways for the power of God to flow, but also breaks the power of the enemy over your life and the lives of those for which you intercede.

Fast in faith with determined purpose. Be aware of the power fasting produces. As you pray, take hold of the promise of God by faith and be determined to obtain it. Many people fast but do not have a clue as to the power they are tapping into. Therefore, they do not realize the same results they would if they were aware of all that transpires in the realm of the Spirit as they fast. Fasting without faith and focus is simply doing without food. God honors the effort, but there is much more available.

Fasting sharpens your focus on Jesus Christ. If you are not careful, food will dull your spiritual perception. When you overload your stomach, your spirit becomes dull and you lose sight of your true purpose.

The fullness and prosperity you have obtained carries the potential to cause you to forget your purpose. Christians are sometimes willing to seek God until they get their blessing, but they have a tendency to forget where their blessing came from. Beware that you do not forget the Lord and His work in the days of your prosperity. In good times, continue to pray, fast and seek God's will and desire. God uses fasting to enlighten the eyes of your heart and to draw you close to Him.

FASTING IN FAITH WITH DETERMINED PURPOSE

Isaiah 58 is a favorite chapter of mine. It is a type of biblical *outline* for fasting and gives guidelines of what true fasting *is* and what it *is not*. This chapter defines the accomplishments you attain when you fast with the right motives and purpose. It is a *faith-building, promise-packed,* and *purpose-filled* chapter. While fasting, I use **Isaiah 58** as a prayer tool. You and I will experience *all* of the promises in **Isaiah 58** if we follow the guidelines in this chapter.

Isaiah 58:1-5

"Cry aloud, spare not, lift up thy voice like a trumpet, and shew my people their transgression, and the house of Jacob their sins. Yet they seek me daily, and delight to know my ways, as a nation that did righteousness, and forsook not the ordinance of their

God: they ask of me the ordinances of justice; they take delight in approaching to God. Wherefore have we fasted, say they, and thou seest not?wherefore have we afflicted our soul, and thou takest no knowledge? Behold, in the day of your fast ye find pleasure, and exact all your labours. Behold, ye fast for strife and debate, and to smite with the fist of wickedness: ye shall not fast as ye do this day, to make your voice to be heard on high. Is it such a fast that I have chosen?a day for a man to afflict his soul? is it to bow down his head as a bulrush, and to spread sackcloth and ashes under him? wilt thou call this a fast, and an acceptable day to the Lord?"

Isaiah 58 begins by outlining things that *do not* constitute a true fast. When you afflict *(or cause pain or suffering to)* your soul to attract God and then complain that God does not listen, when you do your own pleasures, and exact *(or urgently do)* all your labors, you are not fasting for the right reasons. If you fast for strife and debate, to make your voice heard, or bow your head to make an impression on others, you are not fasting in the manner God requires. Spreading of sackcloth or ashes will not get God's attention either, only man's.

Matthew 6:16-18

"Moreover when ye fast, be not, as the hypocrites, of a sad countenance: for they disfigure their faces, that they may appear unto men to fast. Verily I say unto you, They have their reward. But thou, when thou fastest, anoint thine head, and wash thy face; That thou appear not unto men to fast, but unto thy Father which is in secret: and thy Father, which seeth in secret, shall reward thee openly."

According to **Matthew 6:16-18**, making a show to be seen of men in fasting *or any practice* is ineffective. The *Word of God* says those who **"disfigure their faces, that they may appear unto men to fast . . . have their reward."** There is a promise that if you anoint your head and wash your face in order that you do not appear **"unto men"** to fast, but only to the **"Father, which is in secret"**, He sees in secret and rewards you openly! The church in America rarely hears what the Bible says about fasting. Build your faith, study the *Word of God* and apply scripture regarding fasting. In your prayer time, while fasting, rehearse the scripture promises to the Lord. As you do, you will hear the promises of God and that is how faith comes.

People fasted throughout the Bible for various purposes. When someone went without food, it was serious. They were seeking an answer from God. Denying your body food tells God you are willing to set aside the needs of your physical body to seek Him for an answer to your problem.

Isaiah 58:6

"Is not this the fast that I have chosen?to loose the bands of wickedness, to undo the heavy burdens, and to let the oppressed go free, and that ye break every yoke?"

When fasting according to God's guidelines, the bands of wickedness will be loosed for you *and* those you are praying for. Heavy burdens will be undone, all concerned will walk free from oppression and every yoke will be broken. Fasting releases a *"yoke destroying"* anointing!

Isaiah 58:7

"Is it not to deal thy bread to the hungry, and that thou bring the poor that are cast out to thy house? When thou seest the naked, that thou cover him; and that thou hide not thyself from thine own flesh?"

It is important that you do not forget to feed the hungry, bring the poor into your house, cover the naked and be available to your own flesh *(family)*. If you fast, but you neglect these important details, your fast is not valid before God.

Isaiah 58:8 says, *"then shall thy light break forth as the morning"*. God promises revelation when you fast. Just as you confidently expect a bright morning after a long night of darkness, you can expect a fast to produce a glittering sunrise of revelation when done according to God's guidelines and purpose.

What makes the morning light so bright is the *darkness* of the night. It may have been dark for a long time, but revelation *will* come. Revelation comes through different avenues. You may find that you suddenly know how to handle a situation you have been dealing with for a long time. A scripture you have read time and time again suddenly comes alive and gives direction. Whatever the avenue, fasting carries the promise to give you revelation that will light your way.

Some people are afraid to fast. They are deceived into thinking fasting will kill them. This is simply *NOT* true. *That* is not what the *Word of God* says! The Bible teaches, according to **Isaiah 58:8**, *"and thine health shall spring forth speedily:"* if you fast, it will not kill you, it will heal you! This means you do not have to suffer for weeks, months, or years with a critical condition threatening your well being. If you are dealing with illness, fast with determined purpose to obtain the promise provided for you. First, receive the promise, then walk in it.

Isaiah 58:8b

"And thy righteousness shall go before thee; the glory of the Lord shall be thy rearward."

When you fast, your flesh is afflicted or *"crucified"* in order for the spirit man inside to shine forth. Others will see your Holy lifestyle. Your life will begin to consistently show forth the Lordship of Jesus Christ.

The glory of the Lord will be your rear protection just as it was for the children of Israel when leaving Egypt.

Exodus 14:20

"And it came between the camp of the Egyptians and the camp of Israel; and it was a cloud and darkness to them, but it gave light by night to these: so that the one came not near the other all the night."

God led them by day and protected them from behind at night (*or when it was dark*). He will do the same for you as you fast.

Isaiah 58:9

"Then shalt thou call, and the LORD shall answer; thou shalt cry, and he shall say, Here I am."

When? Then! When you are fasting with the right motives and with a repentant heart, *then* you will call or pray and will get answers that have not come until now.

Isaiah 58: 9b-10

"If thou take away from the midst of thee the yoke, the putting forth of the finger, and speaking vanity; And if thou draw out thy soul to the hungry, and satisfy the afflicted soul; then shall thy light rise in obscurity, and thy darkness be as the noon day:"

If you stop pointing fingers, speaking vanity, draw out your soul to the hungry and satisfy the afflicted soul, *"THEN shall thy light rise in obscurity, and thy darkness be as the noon day"*. The light of the promise God gave you will rise out of the darkness. People who have never heard of you or paid attention will take notice of your accomplishments for the *Kingdom of God*. No longer will the darkness of *unbelief* shroud the destiny God has outlined for you. Fasting *unveils* and drives out *unbelief*.

The enemy has used *unbelief* to convince you that God has forgotten all the powerful promises he has given you. He wants you to doubt all of the prophecies spoken to you. The devil will try to hide your destiny in the darkness of finger pointing and vain speaking, but those demonic forces are dealt with as you fast.

You may have experienced trouble on every hand. You may feel as though you have fallen into a pit and darkness has swallowed you; but as you *fast in faith, with determined purpose*, to obtain the promise, your darkest hour will be like high noon!

Do you need guidance? You need to fast. It is a promise. If you are faithful to fasting and prayer, **Isaiah 58: 11** says, *"And the LORD shall guide thee continually."* No more uncertainty about the will of God, no more second-guessing what God has spoken, He said He would guide you *continually.* He will *"satisfy your soul in times of drought, and make fat thy bones."* I do not know about you, but my bones are the *only* thing I want *fat* on me!

Isaiah 58:11

"And the Lord shall guide thee continually, and satisfy thy soul in drought, and make fat thy bones: and thou shalt be like a watered garden, and like a spring of water, whose waters fail not."

As you fast, the Lord will satisfy your soul in times of drought and you will be like a *"watered garden"* whose waters fail not. You will have a never-ending supply of fresh life-giving water to draw from. God's provision will always be there in abundance for whatever you need.

Jeremiah 17:7-8
"Blessed is the man that trusteth in the LORD, and whose hope the LORD is. For he shall be as a tree

planted by the waters, and that spreadeth out her roots by the river, and shall not see when heat cometh, but her leaf shall be green; and shall not be careful in the year of drought, neither shall cease from yielding fruit."

As you recognize your total dependence upon the Lord, you become more fruitful and full of life. Fasting will make you keenly aware of who God is and how He will sustain you.

Isaiah 58:12

"And they that shall be of thee shall build the old waste places: thou shalt raise up the foundations of many generations; and thou shalt be called, The repairer of the breach, The restorer of paths to dwell in."

"And they that shall be of thee". . . This may be your children, church congregation, family or friends. There may be a break or rupture in relationships. The ones closest to you may be tearing things down now but the promise through proper fasting is that they will *"build the old waste places"*. They will have a God-given desire to repair, restore, and rebuild the empty, unused, torn down places in their lives and the lives they touch. Through fasting and obedience to the *Word of God*, other people's lives will be repaired, restored, and rebuilt. Those you are praying for while fasting, will find their way back to a relationship with God, which will cause restoration and reconciliation in relationships. Through fasting and prayer you *"raise up the foundations of many generations; and though shalt be called, The repairer of the breach, The restorer of paths to dwell in"*.

The dictionary defines *"breach"* as a *"broken, ruptured, or torn condition or area, a gap in continuity, or an infraction or violation of a law, obligation, standard or tie".* There are torn conditions and gaps in continuity in many lives. Past, current, and future generations have been affected by the destruction of the enemy. This destruction causes many *"breaches".* There may be breaches in relationships with God due to circumstances. There may be breaches in finances due to lost jobs and slow economy. There may be breaches in relationships with family and friends through, offense, death, or misunderstandings. All of these breaches can be instrumental in *veiling unbelief* in the lives of God's people.

The *Word of God* says the foundations of *"many"* generations will rise up through fasting. Faith and obedience to God in fasting reach back into the past, take hold of the promises and change generations.

Do you know people who have served the Lord or worked in ministry and have fallen by the wayside? You will be instrumental in the restoration of their lives through fasting and prayer. Through proper fasting, God will help them find the right path and repair the burned and desolate places. Through obedience to God's guidelines for prayer and fasting, their hearts will turn to God. Fasting lays a foundation for growth: a foundation built on solid, godly principles and strength in Him.

Isaiah 58:13

"If thou turn away thy foot from the sabbath, from doing thy pleasure on my holy day; and call the

sabbath a delight, the holy of the LORD, honourable; and shalt honour him, not doing thine own ways, nor finding thine own pleasure, nor speaking thine own words ;

Fasting requires solid commitment. While fasting, making special time for God each day is crucial. Devote yourself to seeking God's face, especially during weak, vulnerable or irritable times. Read His Word and pray during mealtimes. Meditate on the Lord, sing to Him, and make every thing you do an act of praise and worship. True fasting focuses on God and makes Him the center of your words, actions, attitudes and desire.

As you enter times of prayer and fasting, be aware; Satan will do anything possible to pull you away from Bible reading and prayer time. The enemy makes you a target because he knows God has something very special to show you as you wait upon Him and seek His face. The enemy will do *anything* he can to stop you. He will make you hungry, bring up trouble in your family or work and make you irritable in order to sway your focus away from the Lord. When the evil one comes to discourage you, immediately pray and ask God for strength. Take authority over these attacks in Jesus' name.

Isaiah 58:14

"Then shalt thou delight thyself in the LORD; and I will cause thee to ride upon the high places of the earth, and feed thee with the heritage of Jacob thy father: for the mouth of the LORD hath spoken it."

If you fast, your delight will turn from the things of this world to God. When this happens, He promised to *"cause you to ride upon the high places of the earth"*. No longer will you be down, crawling and scratching, attempting to eek by. He will *cause* you to ride. It takes little to no effort to ride, but a great deal of effort to crawl. God will lift you from your lowly, struggling, crawling, scratching position and bring you up where the ride is smooth, but you must fast according to God's guidelines.

A greater sensitivity to spiritual things and renewed closeness with God are benefits of fasting. If you do not, immediately see outward results, do not despair, be disappointed or discouraged. If you have honestly sought God's face, rest assured He is working on your behalf to make necessary changes. If you have set yourself to fast, and have completed the fast unto Him as an act of worship, according to His guidelines of an acceptable fast, God will honor your commitment. You may not see immediate results in the natural realm. Just hold steady, God has been doing undercover work while you were disciplining your flesh and the outward results are sure to manifest.

When you *fast in faith with determined purpose* and your motives are for the accomplishment of the will and glory of God, He will honor and bless you. Again, study your Bible further in the areas of prayer and fasting and allow God to give you personal revelation of each of these extremely important tools of warfare and worship.

SPEAK TO THIS MOUNTAIN

Matthew 17: 20

"And Jesus said unto them, Because of your unbelief: for verily I say unto you, If ye have faith as a grain of mustard seed, ye shall say unto this mountain, Remove hence to yonder place; and it shall remove; and nothing shall be impossible unto you."

Once you have been through the "Mustard Seed Process" and allowed God to develop *"faith as a grain of mustard seed"* or faith that *"acts like"* a grain of mustard seed, *"what next"* you ask. Notice **Matthew 17:20, *"Ye shall say unto this mountain, Remove hence to yonder place; and it shall remove"*.** The Bible does not say, *"ye shall pick up a shovel and start digging"* or *"ye shall start climbing at once"*. The Bible says, ***"Ye shall SAY unto this mountain, remove hence to yonder place."***

It has been established that the mountain being discussed is not a literal mountain, but the spiritual mountain of *"unbelief"*. I have talked about the many ways a mountain of *unbelief* forms, the causes of a mountain of *unbelief*, and the effects of allowing a mountain of *unbelief* to remain. It will literally cause you to forfeit your promise.

Do not allow a mountain of *unbelief* to stand in your way. You are almost there. The race is almost finished and you have almost reached your destiny. This is no time to give up. With that in mind, you need to know the next step in ridding your life of *unbelief* and moving into the vision God has given. The answer is in your speech. Yes! It is in what you say with your mouth!

You have already been through the crushing, dying, sprouting, growing, and developing the root system. You have overcome every obstacle in your path and have determined you will continue to press in for your promise, but what are you *saying* about it? Are you talking about the problem or the solution? Are you spending more time telling everyone what is wrong rather than what will be right in the end? How much of what you say is negative, and how much is the *Word of God*?

It may not have occurred to you that you are talking negatively or not speaking the *Word of God* over problems and circumstances. If you pay attention, you may discover your speech is hindering you from seeing your vision come to pass.

Focus on what you *"say"* with your mouth regarding your problems and circumstances.

Proverbs 18:21

"Death and life are in the power of the tongue: and they that love it shall eat the fruit thereof."

This scripture proves you have power to affect your destiny with words. Death *and* life are in the power of the tongue. You choose to speak life or death. You choose to speak the *Word of God* or speak negatively about the process God is using to bring your vision to pass. Negative statements such as, *"I will never make it through this situation, I cannot take one more thing, this is breaking me, these problems are overtaking me, I am not qualified to do this, I know I will fail, or I cannot take the pressure."* are speaking death.

Do not speak against or question the vision of another person. If you see something that does not seem right, *PRAY.* Ask God for wisdom, direction, and the right words to say if something needs to be said. It is possible to speak negative words to a person who is struggling. Your negative words can set them back or cripple their hope. Concentrate on speaking positive words and speaking the *Word of God* to others. You *must* understand, according to Matthew 12:36, you will be accountable for the words you speak.

Matthew 12:36

"But I say unto you, That every idle word that men shall speak, they shall give account thereof in the day of judgment."

In the Day of Judgment, you will give account for every word *"lacking worth"* or *"not used appropriately"*. This should cause you to desire to be more careful about what you say!

There is power in your tongue. There is mountain-moving power in your mouth or Jesus would not have said you could **"say"** to the mountain **"be removed"**. Speak the *Word of God* to problems and circumstances.

Remember the centurion who said **"Lord, I am not worthy that thou shouldest come under my roof but speak the word only, and my servant shall be healed"**? This centurion knew all he needed was *THE WORD* from Jesus and his servant would be healed. You need no special ceremonies or requirements, only the *Word of God*. This is *all* you need to remove the mountain of *unbelief* hindering you. It is all you need to prevent one from forming. You need to speak the *Word of God* only! When negative thoughts come, rebuke them, and *speak the Word of God*. When negative people rise up, rebuke the spirit operating through them, and *speak the Word of God*. When you find yourself speaking negatively concerning your vision, rebuke doubt and *unbelief* in you and *speak the Word of God*. Speech is a powerful tool and it has a profound effect on both things in the natural *and* in the spirit.

Mark 11: 22-23

> *"And Jesus answering saith unto them, Have faith in God. For verily I say unto you, That whosoever shall say unto this mountain, Be thou removed, and be thou cast into the sea; and shall not doubt in his heart, but shall believe that those things which he saith shall come to pass; he shall have whatsoever he saith."*

Jesus tells His disciples, you can have **whatever you say**! I do not know about you, but there have been some things *I* have said that *I DO NOT* want! *Guard your mouth!*

Proverbs 21:23

> *"Whoso keepeth his mouth and his tongue keepeth his soul from troubles."*

If you speak trouble, then trouble you will receive. If you speak the *Word of God* in every situation, you will see positive results.

170   Faith as...

You will see a mountain of *unbelief* move! When you speak to the mountain, the *Word of God* says *NOTHING SHALL BE IMPOSSIBLE UNTO YOU!*

NOTHING IS IMPOSSIBLE!

If you have *"faith as a grain of mustard seed"*, you can deal with the devil. Jesus said, *"if"* you have *"faith as a grain of mustard seed"* you can speak to the mountain and it will move. It is impossible to live in this earth and not run into a mountain occasionally.

It is vital for you to confront the devil. He will use *unbelief* to delay your destiny, and if he accomplishes this, it will bring him delight. There is a devil assigned to your life to keep your destiny out of reach. The good news is Jesus has an assignment for your life that is far more powerful than the assignment of the devil. Jesus' assignment for you is twofold: *reach* your destiny, and *walk* in it!

Matthew 17:20

"And Jesus said unto them, Because of your unbelief: for verily I say unto you, If ye have faith as a grain of mustard seed, ye shall say unto this mountain, Remove hence to yonder place; and it shall remove; and nothing shall be impossible unto you."

If you go through the process and allow, *"faith as a grain of mustard seed"* to be developed in you *"nothing shall be impossible"*! *NOTHING! NO THING* shall be impossible unto you!

No ministry God has called you to will be unattainable, no matter how unqualified the world says you are. Remember, God says you are glorified!

No family member will remain lost and undone without God or His Son.

No son or daughter will remain in rebellion, drugs, alcohol, sexual promiscuity, or wrong relationships.

No husband who has decided he does not love you and does not want to serve God will remain lost or estranged.

No wife who has decided she married too young and wants out of her marriage is too hard for God to change her thinking.

No supervisor who has decided you are not worthy of promotion will hold you back. God says, *"It is time for promotion"!*

No job opportunity God has placed in your heart will be out of reach.

No attack on the financial prosperity of your business will avail.

No house, no car, and no school you have a desire for will be unattainable.

No ministry broken and in anguish from abuse by people with ulterior motives will remain or continue without reconciliation and restoration.

No sickness will overtake you.

No unhappiness and disunity in your family will prevail.

No integrity will be lost, no matter how many wrong choices you have made. God will restore.

No hopelessness, depression, or despair will maintain a stronghold in you.

No opportunity for success in ministry, employment, or relationships will be lost.

NOTHING! Nothing shall be impossible! *NO THING* shall be impossible if you have fully developed *"Faith AS"* or faith that *"acts like"* a grain of mustard seed!

You can do this! Now that *unbelief* has been *unveiled*, you can walk in the promises of God and see His plan accomplished in your life. You can help others endure the *"Mustard Seed Process"* by which their ***"faith as a grain of mustard seed"*** will be developed. Extend your hand to those experiencing the difficult but necessary process that develops ***"faith as a grain of mustard seed"*** or faith that *"acts like"* a grain of mustard seed. As you do this, you are maturing spiritually and making considerable contribution to the body of Christ!

Ephesians 4:15-16

"But speaking the truth in love, may grow up into him in all things, which is the head, even Christ: From whom the whole body fitly joined together and compacted by that which every joint supplieth, according to the effectual working in the measure of every part, maketh increase of the body unto the edifying of itself in love."

Grow together and help each person placed in your path to reach their destiny. If you see a mountain of *unbelief* forming in the life of your brother or sister, share with them what you have learned about *"faith as a grain of mustard seed"* or faith that *"acts like"* a grain of mustard seed.

Press in, push forward, and remove the mountain of *unbelief.* Allow Jesus to mine the gems buried deep in your mountain, and move on to finish the race, and reach your destiny.

When *"faith as a grain of mustard seed"* or faith that *"acts like"* a grain of mustard seed is fully developed and you speak to the mountain of *unbelief,* it will move to yonder place and you will advance freely to accomplish God's vision for your life and reach your destiny.

UNVEILING UNBELIEF – CONCLUSION

The material presented in this book has been shared with you in hope that you will hide these words in your heart and deal with the mountain of *unbelief* in you as it is *unveiled* by the Holy Spirit.

Some will take hold of the concepts discussed and confront *unbelief* until it is completely dealt with.

Sadly, some will *attempt* to take hold; but when trouble comes, as trouble does, they will be tempted to do what they have always done-*quit!* My prayer is that *all* will break out of the cycle of giving-up, press into the principles of God, and develop the *"faith as a grain of mustard seed"* needed to finish the race and fulfill their *God-given destiny.*

Some will be unwilling to do all it takes to develop faith and deal with the mountain of *unbelief.* Thank God for those who *will.* If it takes a fast, they will fast. If it takes two fasts, they will fast twice.

They will discipline themselves in prayer and speaking the *Word of God* over situations and circumstances.

It is my estimation that anyone who does not desire *"mustard seed faith"* to be developed in them is either, *misinformed, uninformed,* or *chloroformed*. They are **misinformed** concerning what is restraining them from accomplishing their vision, **uninformed** of the power available after the *process* develops *"mustard seed faith"* or **chloroformed** *(or anesthetized)* to all hope of realizing the accomplishment of the vision God gave long ago.

Be determined to enter into what God has promised. Concerning your destiny, *you will make it, if you can take it!* Seriously consider this information. Every word is important. If God said it, *BELIEVE* it and *BELIEVE FOR IT! Confront unbelief!*

I am reaching out to people who are determined to develop *"faith as a grain of mustard seed"* and who are determined to deal with their mountain of *unbelief.*

I am reaching out to people who are determined to finish the race and fulfill their *God-given destiny.*

Be strengthened! Be encouraged! GOD IS IN CONTROL!
I leave you with this blessing.

Numbers 6:24-26 (NKJV).

"The Lord bless you and keep you; The Lord make his face to shine upon you and be gracious to you; the Lord look upon you with favor and give you peace."